Groundhog
Day

ALSO BY DON YODER

Amish Folk Medicine
(with Barbara Duncan)

Discovering American Folklife

The Picture-Bible of Ludwig Denig

Hex Signs
(with Thomas E. Graves)

Rhineland Emigrants

Pennsylvania German Immigrants

American Folklife

Pennsylvania Spirituals

Songs along the Mahantongo
(with Walter E. Boyer and Albert F. Buffington)

Groundhog Day

Don Yoder

STACKPOLE
BOOKS

Published by
STACKPOLE BOOKS
5067 Ritter Road
Mechanicsburg, PA 17055
www.stackpolebooks.com

Punxsutawney Phil® is a registered trademark of the Punxsutawney Groundhog Club.

Printed in the United States of America

10 9 8 7 6 5 4 3 2 1

FIRST EDITION

Design by Beth Oberholtzer

Frontispiece: *Punxsutawney Phil and his handler, Bill Deeley.*
PUNXSUTAWNEY GROUNDHOG CLUB INNER CIRCLE

Library of Congress Cataloging-in-Publication Data

Yoder, Don.
    Groundhog Day / Don Yoder.—1st ed.
       p.   cm.
    ISBN 0-8117-0029-1 (hc)
    1. Groundhog Day.   I. Title.
GT4995.G76Y63   2003
394.261–dc21

                                             2003014344

TO MY SISTER MARY

Who like myself was born and raised in the
Groundhog Country of Central Pennsylvania

CONTENTS

PREFACE

From the Pennsylvania Dutch Country in Southeastern and Central Pennsylvania has spread, during the past two centuries, the fun holiday celebration of Groundhog Day. It is one of the many gifts of the Pennsylvania Dutch to our nation, along with the Conestoga wagon, the bank barn, and the Lancaster rifle, yes, and scrapple, Lebanon bologna, and shoofly pie.

Now firmly ensconced as a national event every February 2, it radiates outward from Punxsutawney, Pennsylvania, self-styled "Weather Capital of the World," where the sage prognosticating Groundhog, Punxsutawney Phil, has become a national icon. Today the Groundhog Day map includes such far-flung outposts as Wisconsin, where Jimmy the Sun Prairie Groundhog does the honors; Ohio, the realm of Buckeye Chuck; and Georgia, where little General Beauregard Lee waddles out from his white-columned plantation mansion to sniff the air and see if his shadow is available. Many other places have Groundhog Day activities—Vermont, Louisiana, even Ontario and Nova Scotia—and each year additional spots light up on the map.

Groundhog Day derives from ancient, undoubtedly prehistoric, weather lore. It revolves around the time-honored folk belief, brought here from Europe, that if the Groundhog (in Germany a badger or earlier the sacred bear) leaves his hibernation chamber and sees his shadow, he predicts or prognosticates, as the media have it, six more weeks of winter, to the unanimous groans of top-hatted votaries standing around shivering in the cold dawn air.

The Groundhog Day cult gives us all a welcome holiday to celebrate between New Year's Day and Easter, and in doing so, provides us with a bit of fantasy and lots of festivity—something all of us need occasionally in our everyday workaday world. May the day and its festivities keep spreading!

It has been great fun writing this book. It introduced me and will introduce you to the complicated history of the celebration, from its origins as the midwinter turning point of the year, as marked by our Celtic ancestors all over Western Europe and the British Isles. The book also introduces the Groundhog as a vital if tongue-in-cheek symbol of the Pennsylvania Dutch. This identity is celebrated in the all-dialect *Grundsow Lodges* (Groundhog Lodges) of Southeastern Pennsylvania, where every February hundreds of Dutchmen meet to spend the evening feasting and frolicking, with pledges of allegiance, the sacred Groundhog Oath, and lots of harmless revelry—all in Pennsylvania Dutch.

You will learn too from these pages how journalists shaped the holiday and helped it spread with their enthusiastic reports, so that today television cameras are focused on Punxsutawney, Quarryville, and all the other hot spots on the Groundhog Day map. Bill Murray's charming film, *Groundhog Day*, helped give the holiday national recognition. And a procession of clever writers has created several dozen winsome children's storybooks about the Groundhog and his day.

Through this holiday, the Groundhog has in a sense been personalized and humanized. It has also helped us humans to recognize our relation to the natural environment. So if you see a shy Groundhog or hear him whistling out in the woods or fields, be nice to him. On February 2, he'll predict for you whether there will be six more weeks of winter or an early spring.

Don Yoder
Groundhog Day 2003

ACKNOWLEDGMENTS

In writing this book, I have received the help of many colleagues, assorted persons whose works deserve citation, and a multitude of institutions—libraries, historical societies, ethnic organizations, and newspapers.

I have combed the research libraries of Philadelphia and Eastern Pennsylvania for Groundhog material. In the Metropolitan area, I wish to thank the Library Company of Philadelphia and the libraries of the University of Pennsylvania, Haverford College, Chester County Historical Society, and Tredyffrin Township. Farther afield, thanks go to the Historical Society of Berks County, York County Heritage Trust, Spruance Library of the Bucks County Historical Society, Pennsylvania State Library in Harrisburg, and the library of my own alma mater, Franklin and Marshall College.

Ethnic organizations whose collections and publications have aided my research include the Pennsylvania German Society, the Pennsylvania German Cultural Heritage Center at Kutztown University, and the various Groundhog Lodges of the Pennsylvania Dutch Country. To the principal coordinator of the lodges at the present time, Carl D. Snyder of New Tripoli in Lehigh County—longtime friend whom I have known for half a century—I extend cordial thanks for his help. He generously provided me with historic lodge programs and rare photographs of the doings of the oldest of the lodges, *Grundsow Lodge Nummer Ains an der Lechaw* (Groundhog Lodge Number One on the Lehigh River), which has been going strong since its founding in 1934.

Punxsutawney, Pennsylvania, the acknowledged capital of the Groundhog Day movement, deserves lots of thanks expressed to specific individuals who kindly and courteously supported my project and furnished photos, information, and enthusiasm. The Punxsutawney Chamber of Commerce has been especially helpful, and here I thank Kerry Presloid in particular. Punxsutawney Phil's genial handler, Bill Deeley, whose million-dollar smile appears on the jacket of this book, was always willing to talk over the phone with me when I needed his input. Bill Cooper, president of the Punxsutawney Groundhog Club Inner Circle, provided helpful knowledge. Tom Curry, director of the Punxsutawney Area Historical and Genealogical Society, has been extremely forthcoming in responding to my requests for information about the founder of the Punxsutawney Groundhog Day event, Clymer H. Freas. The Adrian Hospital gave instant permission to reproduce the classic recipe for cooking groundhog that originally appeared in *Cooking with the Groundhog*. And Bill Anderson, through his fabulous book, *Groundhog Day, 1886 to 1992: A Century of Tradition in Punxsutawney, Pennsylvania*, has pointed me many times in the right direction.

Pennsylvania's second venue of Groundhog Day festivity, Quarryville, in Lancaster County, has responded with information and illustrations. Dr. James E. Pennington, the obliging chairman of the Board of Hibernating Governors, has generously sent me lodge programs and photographs and given me insights that have helped my interpretation. Douglas Withers Groff's literally immense (690-page!) opus, *The Slumbering Groundhog Lodge of Quarryville, Pennsylvania, in the Twentieth Century*, has furnished me with the historical basis for the Quarryville story. Thanks to Doug Groff for materials substantive and pictorial.

For the development of Groundhog Day outside Pennsylvania, I am indebted to the chambers of commerce of Sun Prairie, Wisconsin; Marion, Ohio; and Lilburn, Georgia; as well as the informative website of the Committee for the Commercialization of Groundhog Day, groundhogsday.com.

Newspapers—the cutting-edge record of what goes on in the world—have aided immensely in rounding out the picture of how Groundhog Day has come to be celebrated in the United States. My thanks go first to the venerable Punxsutawney *Spirit* and its publisher, Mary Jude Troupe, for permission to use materials on the early history of Groundhog Day. Other newspapers deserve thanks. My hometown newspaper, the Altoona *Mirror*, always provided good coverage of Groundhog Day and the Punxsutawney festivities. The Allentown *Morning Call* and the Lehigh County weekly, *Parkland and Northwestern Press*, have furnished coverage of the Groundhog Lodge activities by such writers as Richard Druckenbrod and David Semmel. In addition, I mention with thanks the Levittown *Courier-Times*, Doylestown *Intelligencer*, Schuylkill County *Citizen-Standard*, Pittsburgh *Post-Gazette*, Lancaster *New Era*, Reading *Times*, and Reading *Eagle*.

And finally, some personal notices. Many thanks to my diligent editor, Kyle R. Weaver, of Stackpole Books, for constant support, prodding, and countless refinements to the text. Thanks also to Kyle for accompanying me on my research trip to Punxsutawney, where we experienced firsthand the festivity of the Groundhog Day event in all its glory.

To J. M. Duffin, former student and now assistant archivist at the University of Pennsylvania, thanks for courteous surfings of the Internet for missing dates, publishers, and other embarrassing gaps in my text.

To William Woys Weaver, my thanks for being there when I needed stylistic improvements and overviews from his wide-ranging research.

To John and Jan Haigis for the use of their charming Groundhog Day carols, deep thanks and appreciation for their labor of love for our holiday.

To photographer George W. Powers, thanks for the privilege of using the matchless photograph of Phil and Bill that adorns our jacket.

To Prof. Stam Zervanos of the Penn State Reading campus, my thanks for sharing essential scientific data, not available elsewhere, on nature's groundhog.

To my cousin, Don Myers, of Philipsburg, thanks for his reminiscences on hunting and eating groundhog in Centre County, and also to Jane Waite Stover, of Greensburg, for similar memories of her growing-up days in the Allegheny Mountain country.

My thanks also to an unforgettable student, the late Hilda Adam Kring, one of the many doctoral children whom I had the good fortune to instruct during my years at the University of Pennsylvania. Her materials on Mary Goes over the Mountain, St. Swithin's Day, and St. Mary of the Snows were researched under my direction in my classes in folk religion.

My deep gratitude goes to my sister, Mary Yoder Miller, of Altoona, for checking facts and publications in the local libraries and providing me with useful newspaper clippings. I dedicate this book to Sister Mary, with gratitude for her affection over the decades and her loyalty to family and the Central Pennsylvania tradition.

CHAPTER I

Groundhog Day in Punxsutawney

It was cold, bitter cold, on Gobbler's Knob at 3 A.M. on February 2, 2002, when we got out of the car at the press parking lot and headed for the action at the main stage. And there was action already—several barefoot karate experts dressed in white oriental robes were chopping boards and unfolding their legs into the air at striking angles, all to the accompaniment of loud recordings of rock music, which would continue until dawn, when the music became patriotic and sentimental.

Gobbler's Knob, the sacred gathering place of American Ground-hogism each February 2, is a large hill outside of Punxsutawney, pleasantly dotted with tall trees like a camp-meeting grove or summertime picnic ground. The focus of attention, the main stage, stands at the center of a semi-circular declivity that forms a natural amphitheater. The ground all over the Knob was covered with a layer of hay to shield attendees from the underlying mud, but in the frigid weather the mud was frozen solid.

The crowds were already arriving and filling the onlookers' space. As press and special guests, my editor and I could stand directly in front of the platform, where we could see everything and record the proceedings. The karate choppers left, and for the next four hours—till dawn and the awakening of Punxsutawney Phil—various groups of enthusiastic Ground-hoggers, mostly college students, danced and cavorted on the stage, among them several groups of boys stripped to the waist in the piercing cold.

The stage at Gobbler's Knob, shortly after 3:00 A.M., when the festivities begin.
KYLE R. WEAVER

In his Inner Circle top hat, the emcee greeted each group and periodically asked students from colleges in various states to identify themselves. He also called to the audience in folk festival fashion, "Are you happy?" "Are you cold?" and various other amusing calls, all enthusiastically answered by shouts from all over the hill.

Amusing signs proliferated, held up by enthusiastic spectators. "We love Phil—Let It Snow" was one; "Phil Is A-1 02-02-02," said another; and best of all, "Here 15 Years and Can't Get my 'Phil.'" Among the performers on stage was an Elvis Presley imitator, mingling American popular culture with the folk culture of Groundhog Day.

Over to one side, a huge brush and log fire had been kindled. The fire reminded the historian in me of the great festal fires lighted on the hills by our pre-Christian Celtic forefathers in Europe on the turning points of their calendar year: November 1, February 1, May 1, and August 1. We walked over to it to gather some warmth in the bitter cold. It was surrounded by numerous attendees with the same idea, but the site was too smoky, so we headed back to the car to recover from the cold. While we thawed out in the car, we could hear everything that was going on at the stage. Once we had warmed up, we ventured forth from our shelter and began exploring again. A snack shanty was serving hot coffee and soup, but the line was too long.

Phil fans wave signs and shout the Groundhog's name. KYLE R. WEAVER

This was a festival indeed! Everyone was dressed for it—quilted coats and stocking caps were everywhere—and everyone was friendly and courteous. I directed some pity toward the 38,000 attendees who weren't allowed to drive to the Knob but had to ride schoolbuses from town, a line of which constantly discharged passengers. These revelers had no refuge from the cold, and thousands of them stood out in it for over four hours.

Things speeded up as the dawning of Groundhog Day approached. Just before dawn, there was a fifteen-minute display of the fanciest fireworks I have seen in years—glorious stars of brilliant color bursting just over our heads, rockets shooting into the heavens and forming striking designs. As the sky grew lighter, the music changed to herald the main event—the summoning of Punxsutawney Phil from his burrow for his annual meteorological prophecy. I turned and looked at the now fully gathered audience filling the natural amphitheater—a magnificent sight indeed.

Now the formal Groundhog Ceremony began. Down the privileged fenced pathway marched in formal procession the Inner Circle, top-hatted, frock-coated Punxsutawney officials and business leaders. They mounted the stage and all were introduced personally, along with their mostly humorous titles. Bill Anderson, Phil's Official Scribe, is publisher

Some of the forty thousand people who traveled to Punxsutawney to see Phil give his forecast. PUNXSUTAWNEY GROUNDHOG CLUB INNER CIRCLE

Phil and the Inner Circle take the stage. PUNXSUTAWNEY GROUNDHOG CLUB INNER CIRCLE

of *Hometown Punxsutawney* magazine and other Pennsylvania newspapers, as well as author of *Groundhog Day 1886 to 1992: A Century of Tradition in Punxsutawney, Pennsylvania* (1992). Bill Cooper is President, and the genial Bill Deeley is Phil's Handler, who presents the animal to the assembled multitudes each year. In addition, there are the Cloud

Card listing the members of the Punxsutawney Groundhog Club Inner Circle. PUNXSUTAWNEY GROUNDHOG CLUB INNER CIRCLE

Builder, Fog Spinner, Storm Chaser, Big Flake Maker, Dew Dropper, Iceman, Stump Warden, Head Hailmaker, and Burrow Master.

The official Groundhog Handler, Bill Deeley, now opened the ceremonial cage and held up the fat, lethargic Phil, who looked around weakly, saw forty thousand pairs of eyes staring at him, and undoubtedly wished

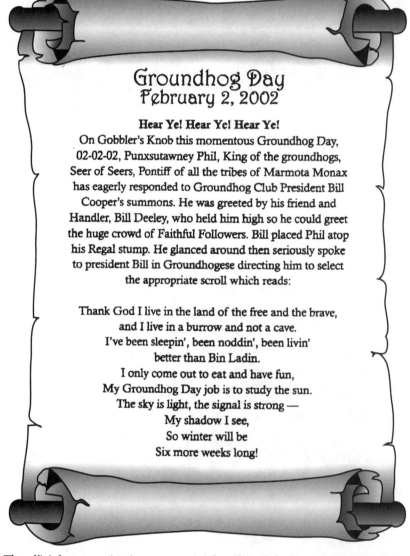

Groundhog Day
February 2, 2002

Hear Ye! Hear Ye! Hear Ye!
On Gobbler's Knob this momentous Groundhog Day,
02-02-02, Punxsutawney Phil, King of the groundhogs,
Seer of Seers, Pontiff of all the tribes of Marmota Monax
has eagerly responded to Groundhog Club President Bill
Cooper's summons. He was greeted by his friend and
Handler, Bill Deeley, who held him high so he could greet
the huge crowd of Faithful Followers. Bill placed Phil atop
his Regal stump. He glanced around then seriously spoke
to president Bill in Groundhogese directing him to select
the appropriate scroll which reads:

Thank God I live in the land of the free and the brave,
and I live in a burrow and not a cave.
I've been sleepin', been noddin', been livin'
better than Bin Ladin.
I only come out to eat and have fun,
My Groundhog Day job is to study the sun.
The sky is light, the signal is strong —
My shadow I see,
So winter will be
Six more weeks long!

The official prognostication, appropriately political, for Groundhog Day 2002.
PUNXSUTAWNEY GROUNDHOG CLUB INNER CIRCLE

Phil mugs for the cameras after making his prediction. KYLE R. WEAVER

he were back in his burrow. But the ritual began. A paper was held before his snout, and the hero of the day saw his shadow.

In "Groundhogese," or so it goes, Phil communicated his message to the world, which was translated into English and formally read out by one of the top-hatted Inner Circle. This year it was a patriotic message, and to accompany it, the "Star-Spangled Banner" was sung, top hats removed. Thus the rite was concluded.

In the morning sun, now fully up, many of the attendees walked down the hills to the town of Punxsutawney rather than wait for the buses. We headed for our motel some twenty miles north, at DuBois in Clearfield County, the nearest we could get to Groundhogtown, for a generous and enjoyable buffet in a pleasantly warm breakfast room.

The Weather Capital of the World

Punxsutawney is a smallish town, with a little over six thousand inhabitants, up in the woods on the Allegheny Plateau in Northwestern Pennsylvania. When you drive west on Interstate 80 over those magnificent mountains, you pass an important watershed: The streams to the east flow into Chesapeake Bay, those to the west flow into the Ohio and the

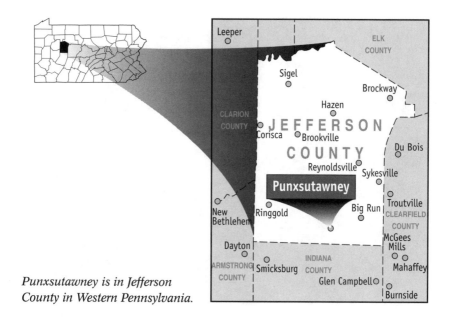

Punxsutawney is in Jefferson County in Western Pennsylvania.

Mississippi, and their waters eventually reach the Gulf of Mexico. And then you reach DuBois—formerly Rumbargertown, named for pioneer settler John Rumbarger, a Pennsylvania Dutchman from Huntingdon County. DuBois is the turnoff point for Punxsutawney, twenty miles away.

Punxsutawney has what many consider an unpronounceable and unspellable name that derives from words in the local Indian language meaning "place of the sand flies." This gave rise to its nickname of "Gnat-Town" when rival towns thought it was getting too uppity. The locals affectionately abbreviate the name to "Punxsy," even in advertising. But whatever it is called, Punxsutawney is known all over Pennsylvania and the nation as "Groundhog Town," the "Weather Capital of the World," and the official residence of the fabulous Punxsutawney Phil, who never fails to prophesy the weather on February 2.

Punxsutawney is in Jefferson County, a division of the Commonwealth of Pennsylvania established as a political community in 1804 and named for then president Thomas Jefferson. This county, along with the entire northwestern corner of the state, was at that time frontier territory, still in the process of settlement. And it took a long time for the area to be settled.

Jefferson and its adjoining counties of Armstrong, Clarion, and Indiana formed a strong Pennsylvania Dutch enclave in Northwestern Pennsylvania. Many of these settlers came before the Civil War from the Mahantongo Valley area of Schuylkill and Northumberland Counties, and from the adjoining areas of northern Dauphin County, particularly the Lykens Valley. In these northwestern sister counties Pennsylvania Dutch customs were planted, and various settlements in the four counties were centers of Pennsylvania Dutch dialect speech up into the 1930s, when several now famous Dutch Jubilee picnics were held, for which the broadside poster advertisements were entirely in the Pennsylvania Dutch language. And among the traditional lore that the Jefferson County Dutchmen brought with them across the mountains from the Dutch Country of Eastern Pennsylvania was that of Groundhog Day.

Today it would be difficult to locate any speakers of Pennsylvania Dutch in the area, except for elderly people who grew up in Dutch-speaking households. But the area is still beautiful. The Mahoning River runs through Punxsutawney, and the river valley towns of the area, such as Big Run, Red Mill, Battle Hollow, Clover Run (groundhogs revel in clover), Desire, and Green Valley, have nostalgic charm with their white frame houses and tall-spired churches. There are farms along the main roads, but because of the surrounding woodlands, Jefferson County is great hunting country, and hunting season is a favorite time of year for the county's menfolk. Groundhogs, beware!

Punxsutawney Borough, with a population of 6,271 according to the 2000 U.S. Census, is a prototypical middle-size American town. It is like hundreds of others in Pennsylvania, a front-porch and backyard-garden town with its rural and woodland surroundings. The population of the greater Punxsutawney area is 20,619, and of Jefferson County, 49,932, again according to the 2000 census figures. In recent years, the borough has become a university town, housing the Punxsutawney campus of Indiana University of Pennsylvania, which includes the Academy of Culinary Arts.

The Evolution of Groundhog Day

The Groundhog Day celebration in Punxsutawney has been traced back to at least the year 1886, when the local newspaper, the *Spirit*, referred to February 2 as "Groundhog Day," saying, "although up to the time of going to press the beast has not seen its shadow." The first Groundhog Picnic,

Clymer Freas

Who was Clymer Freas, the major shaper of Punxsutawney's early Groundhog Day celebration and in effect creator of Pennsylvania's entire groundhog mystique? He was born in Porter Township, Jefferson County, in 1867, to a Pennsylvania Dutchman, Jesse B. Freas, and his Irish-born wife.

This particular branch of the Freas family was evidently planted in America by emigrant ancestor Martinus Fries, who arrived at Philadelphia on October 4, 1751, on the ship *Queen of Denmark*, sailing from Rotterdam and touching at Cowes on the Isle of Wight before heading across the Atlantic.

Clymer Freas's great-grandfather, John Freas (1762–1844), served in the American Revolution from Sussex County, New Jersey. After the war, he moved to Upper Mount Bethel Township, Northampton County, Pennsylvania, where he married Dorcas Hoffman. In 1795, they moved across the mountains to Briar Creek, near Berwick in what is now Columbia County, in the valley of the North Branch of the Susquehanna River. They bought a heavily forested tract, and it is reported that while the settler was clearing enough land for a few fields and space for a log cabin, they lived in their covered wagon. The Indians were evidently still a problem, and when alarms were sounded, the little family fled to Fort Jenkins. John and Dorcas Freas are buried at the Stone Church at Briar Creek.

Clymer's grandfather and Jesse's father, Henry Freas (1798–1877), settled in Red Bank Township, Armstrong County, in 1822, moving to near Ringgold, Jefferson County, in 1834. The area was then a forested wilderness, and Henry bought a tract of about five hundred acres, for which he paid $2 an acre. In the course of time, this was divided into four separate farms. With his first and second wives, Hannah Huntsinger and Susanna Hilliard, Henry Freas had seventeen children, some of whom scattered as far as Rhode Island, Kansas, and Nebraska. Two of his sons, Capts. Jacob Freas and Phillip Freas, served with distinction in the 105th Pennsylvania Regiment during the Civil War.

involving the feasting on groundhog, took place in 1887. So step by step the groundhog celebration evolved, along with the statewide, now nationwide, reputation of Punxsutawney as Groundhog Town.

The Punxsutawney Groundhog Club was organized in 1899, the brainchild of a character (in the best sense of that word) named Clymer H. Freas (1867–1942), then city editor of the Punxsutawney *Spirit*. It was Freas, as a clever and imaginative journalist, who created the Punxsutawney reputation as "Weather Capital," "home" of the Groundhog, and even chose Gob-

Clymer Freas, the father of the Groundhog Day celebration in Punxsutawney. PUNXSUTAWNEY AREA HISTORICAL AND GENEALOGICAL SOCIETY

Clymer Freas attended the country schools in Porter Township and later the Edinboro State Normal School. His brother, Phillip Odessa Freas, served Punxsutawney for many years as burgess, the equivalent of mayor in a borough. Clymer's obituary, which appeared in the Punxsutawney *Spirit* on October 22, 1942, calls him "father of the conception that Punxsutawney is the home of the 'Groundhog.'"

bler's Knob for the Groundhog's annual prognostications. He is credited with creating the recherché language known as "Groundhogese," of which a much-needed dictionary has recently been published. Freas was involved in the very first Groundhog Feast at Punxsutawney in 1899, when Groundhog was festively eaten accompanied by a powerful beverage called Groundhog Punch. To the Groundhog Hunts and Feasts in September, all colorfully reported on by Freas, were added the Groundhog Prophecies on Gobbler's Knob on Candlemas, February 2.

After the turn of the century, the Groundhog Hunts at Punxsutawney became popular and ritualized, attracting devotees from Pittsburgh and elsewhere. For their annual hunt on September 19, 1907, the Punxsutawney and Pittsburgh Groundhog Club wore specially designed badges showing the Groundhog dressed in top hat and bow tie, and carrying in his left paw a huge unfolded umbrella and in his right a bundle of papers marked "Weather for Today." The fact that the umbrella was closed indicated that the day's weather was supposedly, or so it was hoped, fair. The hunt was widely attended, with a special train bringing a delegation from Pittsburgh, led by three colonels, probably all Civil War veterans. Other groups zeroed in from Reynoldsville, DuBois, Big Run, Indiana, and other towns in the Punxsutawney vicinity. It was reported that "the scouts have already rounded up a score of woodchucks, and the prospects are that the feast which will mark the close of the day's hunt will be a notable one." All this was dutifully reported in the *Spirit* on September 19, 1907.

The reputation of Punxsutawney as Groundhog Town was further promoted—again by Clymer Freas, Secretary and Poet Laureate of the Groundhog Club—in a sensational Old Home Week in August 1909. This was a festive week of parades, circus and vaudeville performances, baseball games, class reunions, and fireworks, all of which led up to Friday, August 27, which was dubbed Groundhog Day. On this day, the high point of the week's celebration, the Punxsutawney Groundhog Club staged a magnificent mile-long parade appropriately called the Circumgyratory Pageant of the Astrologers, Horoscopists, Magicians, Soothsayers, and Meteorological Attachés of the Punxsutawney Weather Works. Magnificent floats represented the four seasons, and the "57 Varieties of Weather" (a veiled salute to Pittsburgh?), including snow, sleet, hail, rain, blizzards, squalls, and floods. It was no wonder that the Philadelphia *North American* reported that Groundhog Day was the obvious pièce de résistance of Old Home Week.

The town was honored on this day by the presence of Governor Edwin S. Stuart, Judge John P. Elkin of the Supreme Court, and Congressman John K. Tener (later governor). Clymer Freas, enthusiastic and hyperbolic as ever, describes in the *Spirit*'s columns the Governor's Banquet held after the Circumgyratory Parade:

> The guests once seated were not long in disposing of the menu until groundhog à la Punxsutawney and groundhog punch à la Doc Hughes appeared on the bill. Congressman John K. Tener and Supreme Court Jus-

tice John P. Elkin, in the order named, also exhibited diplomacy in eulogizing the flesh of the only simon pure [vegetarian] on this planet, and
each, under the subtle influence of partaken woodchuck and assimilated
punch grew eloquent and combed the earth, sea and sky with metaphor
and simile, couched in the most beautiful phraseology.

Leigh Mitchell Hodges, the brilliant Philadelphia orator, optimist and
gifted writer of the *North American,* in his eulogy on the newly-elevated
national mascot simply tossed aside all barriers to his well-known storehouse of polished oratory and in one of the most eloquent speeches ever
heard in this city lauded what he had consumed to the realms of scientific
investigation. . . . His address was one climax of grandiloquence after
another culminating in a rhetorical gem to wit: "I consider this banquet
the greatest gastronomical event since the time Adam and Eve attended
that decollate function in the Garden of Eden."

Mr. Hodges's subsidence occurred amid prolonged cheering after he
stated that if he should never eat another bite of groundhog the impressions made upon his gastronomical organs by that which he had already
eaten would remain undimmed as long as life should last.

This unique banquet was brought to a "happy and illustrious conclusion" at 1:15 A.M., with the final speech by the Hon. J. N. Langham, congressman of the Punxsutawney district.

The records of the Punxsutawney Groundhog Club include a listing of
"Phil's Past Predictions (Since 1887)," when he first saw his shadow on
Gobbler's Knob. The first front-page coverage of the event came in 1908.
In 1911, fifty-five couples attended the Groundhog Day Dance, and in
1913, a new dance, the Groundhog Roll, was demonstrated. It appears
that the Punxsutawney Groundhog was not always named Phil; in 1915,
the Prognosticator bore the name of Wiley William Woodchuck. In 1928,
the Groundhog Day event was broadcast on KDKA radio, from Pittsburgh.
In 1940, the Groundhog was photographed with the first Groundhog Day
Queen. In 1952 came the first appearance of Frau Groundhog on "The
Dave Garroway Show" on NBC. In 1958, the Groundhog prepared for
blastoff in his "Chucknik" spacecraft. In 1960, he made the "Today" show,
and in 1962, he was reported as having returned from his second trip to
the moon. In 1986, Punxsutawney Phil made a state visit to President Reagan in the White House. In 1987, he celebrated the one-hundredth anniversary of Groundhog Day. In 1993, the film *Groundhog Day,* starring Bill
Murray, was released in time for Phil's prediction, adding immeasurably to

The Movie

After spreading through the media across the country, Groundhog Day finally made it to Hollywood in 1993. The theme of the movie *Groundhog Day*, directed by Harold Ramis, is simple and intentionally monotonous. Comedian Bill Murray plays the part of a weather reporter from a Pittsburgh TV station who travels by van north to Punxsutawney, accompanied by his nerdish cameraman (Chris Elliot), who drives, and his producer (Andie MacDowell), who provides off-and-on love interest throughout the film. The reporter's task is to narrate the Groundhog's prophecy and all the doings on Gobbler's Knob. But unfortunately for his peace of mind, each day as he rises from his bed in one of Punxsutawney's Edwardian mansions, now a sumptuous bed-and-breakfast, it turns out to be Groundhog Day, again, again, and again.

The film is thus an adult fantasy, played for comedy. Several horror scenarios—fantasies or perhaps dream sequences—are included to contrast with the ordinary small-town atmosphere of Punxsutawney and its population. In one of these, the reporter steals Punxsutawney Phil from his keepers and drives away in a stolen truck—with the Groundhog at the steering wheel—pursued by the police, a car full of top-hatted Inner Circlers, and the TV van. The chase ends with the truck, Groundhog, reporter, and all, going over a huge cliff and exploding into flames at the bottom. But next morning, the reporter is up as usual, and the holiday is repeated. The reporter finally breaks this frightening pattern of repetition by deciding to marry his producer and stay in Punxsutawney.

For those who have attended the once-a-year festivities on Gobbler's Knob outside Punxsutawney, it comes as a surprise to see the Groundhog festivities transferred to the main city square, where the Groundhog's prophecy takes place surrounded by a huge crowd of colorfully dressed people, dozens of them dancing in the band pavilion to the tune of the "Pennsylvania Polka."

It's a virtual Punxsutawney that appears on the screen, since the film, for tactical reasons, was actually shot in Woodstock, Illinois. The town is portrayed as a pleasant, old-fashioned town with big front-porch houses;

Phil's reputation and Punxsutawney's national renown. In 2000, he saw his shadow at 7:28 A.M. and announced the dawn of a "new Phillennium." In 2001, the event was broadcast live at Times Square. And in 2003, Phil had the pleasure of meeting Pennsylvania's new governor, former mayor of Philadelphia Ed Rendell.

And so it went, as the event gained national momentum. Today it is a national popular-culture phenomenon, complete with Groundhog Day cards, carols, children's books, and other accoutrements, and it has been projected into all forms of media—radio, television, and film.

The 1993 Harold Ramis film starring Bill Murray brought widespread national attention to Punxsutawney.

wide, tree-shaded streets; and interesting old brick public buildings. The film brought worldwide attention to Punxsutawney and Punxsutawney Phil, and has helped promote the cult of Groundhogism and the holiday of Groundhog Day across the country. The caricaturing of Punxsutawney's solid citizenry, especially the top-hatted Inner Circle, making them almost—but not quite—urban Appalachian hillbillies, is highly exaggerated and all part of the fun.

"Where the Groundhog Grows"

On Groundhog Day 2001, Punxsutawney Phil, as Ambassador for Pennsylvania to the Big Apple, accompanied Governor Tom Ridge—at least on live television on the huge Times Square screen—to New York. Bill Cooper, president of the Punxsutawney Groundhog Club, who interprets Phil's "Groundhogese" prophecy and translates it into English, made the statement, "Groundhogs always like apples, and the bigger the apple, the better!"

Punxsutawney Phil gives his greeting from a postcard. PUNXSUTAWNEY GROUND-HOG CLUB INNER CIRCLE

Phil's TV tour to the Big Apple was sponsored by the state's Department of Tourism, Film, and Marketing. Its purpose was to advertise to the nation Pennsylvania and Pennsylvania's products, including such major national items as Hershey Chocolate, and make trade contacts for the common-wealth. So before Phil made his appearance on the Broadway screen, tourist films of Pennsylvania's mountains and river valleys were projected to a somewhat surprised audience of New Yorkers walking to work before 8 A.M.

Governor Ridge good-humoredly admitted that he felt upstaged by Phil on this occasion but added, "Phil is quite a cultural icon." When Phil's prediction of "six more weeks of winter" was announced, the governor's fifty or so guests groaned. But he was equal to the occasion. "That's good news," he said, "for the ski resorts in northeast and south-central Pennsylvania."

In 2003, Groundhog Day was marked and made especially festive by the state visit paid to Punxsutawney by newly inaugurated Pennsylvania governor Ed Rendell, former mayor of Philadelphia. His visit was the first such gubernatorial honoring of the town and its Groundhog tradition since 1909, when Governor Edwin S. Stuart, also a Philadelphian, attended the great Groundhog Banquet in connection with Punxsutawney's Old Home Week.

Rendell spoke at the Groundhog Banquet on February 1, Groundhog Eve. Accompanied by his wife, Midge, both wearing Groundhog caps and gloves, the governor took part in the early morning festivities at Gobbler's Knob on February 2. Among the chants and signs on the occasion was one electioneering for "Phil for Governor." Phil is probably a Republican, since the Punxsutawney area is typically a rock-ribbed Republican bastion. Democrat Rendell is Pennsylvania's forty-fifth chief executive, and Phil was coaxed out of his hole for the 117th time to make public his yearly weather prognostication.

One of the most recent and spectacular spinoffs of the Punxsutawney Groundhog Day frenzy is the increasing number of couples who come to Phil's Wedding Chapel in the town to be married on Groundhog Day by Mayor John Hallman. In 2001, ten couples were married or renewed their wedding vows. The high point of the day was the wedding of Dick Dollard of Memphis and Sandy Hanlon of Indianapolis, with Sandy's best friend, Linda Stevens, wearing a Groundhog suit as the Groundhog of Honor. "We're doing it for the love of the holiday," Stevens was reported as saying in the *Altoona Mirror*. The group stayed at the town's distinguished old hotel, the Pantall, where the Groundhog of Honor reserved the room used by Bill Murray on his research visit to Punxsutawney for the 1993 film.

Once Groundhog Day proper is over, Punxsutawney continues throughout the year with Groundhog-related events and celebrations, all of which attract locals and tourists. In midsummer, around the July 4 holiday, the weeklong Summer Groundhog Festival is held downtown. Among the highlights are evening shows of free entertainment, a food alley, craft booths and demonstrations, Children's Day, a city garden tour, and a classic cars cruise. Featured also is the Groundhog Festival 5K Race; later in the year comes the Groundhog Fall 50K Race. All of these events are announced in attractive, glossy, poster-size brochures available from the Punxsutawney Area Chamber of Commerce.

As the town's Chamber of Commerce puts it, "Punxsutawney Phil saw the country through five wars, journeyed to the moon, visited the White House and starred in his own major motion picture." Yet in spite of his wide traveling and his other accomplishments, "the century-old Groundhog continues to delight millions with his mystique and charm and shadow-casting magic each February 2nd in Punxsutawney, Pennsylvania . . . the town where the Groundhog grows!"

Punxsutawney Phil invites the world: "Meet me at Gobbler's Knob!" In this invitation to share in what has become "an American tradition," Phil is joined by the Inner Circle of the Punxsutawney Groundhog Club. And to make it official, Phil signed his signature with his pawprint.

CHAPTER II

From Punxsutawney to the World

From its roots in Punxsutawney in the 1880s, the national spread of Groundhog Day lore and custom, accompanied by humor, festivity, and celebration, was a remarkable phenomenon of the twentieth century. Pennsylvania's second major center of the Groundhog Day cult is the town of Quarryville, in southern Lancaster County. The celebration has spread to other Pennsylvania centers, and eventually to many locales across the nation. It continues to grow and spread even more widely in the twenty-first century.

The Quarryville Story

Quarryville, a pleasant rural town in southern Lancaster County, has been, for nearly a century, the principal Groundhog Day competitor of Punxsutawney. On Groundhog Day 1907, a group of leading citizens of Quarryville met and discussed Groundhog lore and made the decision to initiate an observance the next year. They turned to George W. Hensel Jr., local merchant and banker and a widely known Philadelphia newspaper columnist. Hensel organized the Slumbering Groundhog Lodge, which put on the first Quarryville observation on February 2, 1908. The group was small at first, and all the members listed that year bore Pennsylvania Dutch surnames: Fritz, Hensel, Herr, Martin, Rohrer, and Wimer.

George Washington Hensel Jr., founder of the Quarryville Groundhog Day celebration. DOUGLAS WITHERS GROFF COLLECTION

Hensel's career curiously parallels that of Punxsutawney's Clymer Freas. George Washington Hensel Jr. (1866–1943) was a native of Quarryville, son of George W. Hensel Sr. and Anna (Uhler) Hensel. George Sr., of Pennsylvania Dutch background, had come to Quarryville from Maryland in 1837 and founded the town's hardware store. His son took over the business in 1882 at the age of sixteen. He was a brilliant organizer with a charismatic personality.

After serving as post master of Quarryville in the 1890s, he became president of the Quarryville National Bank and entered Democratic politics, serving on county and state committees. But his principal reputation was gained through his newspaper columns, which ran for sixteen years in the Philadelphia *North American* and for twelve years in the *Philadelphia Inquirer,* the latter column called appropriately "Down Lancaster Way." His jottings were frequently picked up and commented on by other editors, and he was even quoted in the halls of Congress.

The Groundhog Day celebration of the Quarryville Slumbering Groundhog Lodge evolved over the years, and the classic format was fully developed by the 1970s. According to the 1971 program, the revelry began shortly after midnight, G.S.T. (Groundhog Standard Time), when the Observation Squads surveyed the appropriate neighborhood holes for groundhog activity, accompanied by Jimmy the Fiddler playing "Me and My Shadow."

The official call to the Brethren, sent out by the Select and Sapient Secretary in the name of the Board of Hibernating Governors, reads as follows:

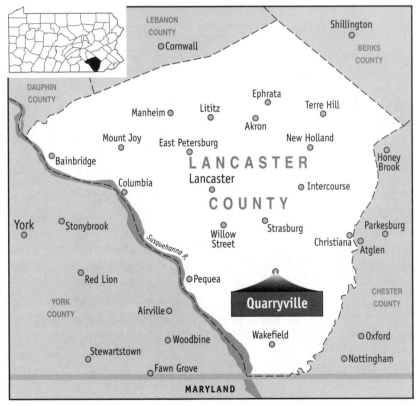

Quarryville is in southern Lancaster County in Southeastern Pennsylvania.

Brethren in full knowledge and enlightenment, Greetings:

By command of the Hibernating Governors and His Excellency the Defender of the Faith, I call all patriarchs, prophets, potentates and pot-bellied Groundhogs, together with all your retinue, to assemble at 9:00 A.M., G.S.T., February 2, next, with proper reverence, humility and solemnity, to do honor to the Prophet of Prophets and to communicate to a waiting world his message which he gives to you in silent eloquence. This summons means you shall put aside all manner of public, private, and personal business, and consecrate yourself and all your worldly possessions to the emulation of the greatness, grandeur and glory of the Most Infallible Prophet Groundhog.

It should not be necessary to remind any self-respecting Slumberer to adorn himself with proper attire—night shirt, top hat and jewels of the faith. In compassion for those hazy in memory or dilatory in mind, it is only fair to warn you and avoid a pyrotechnic penalty. Nothing is so inescapable as a Groundhog's wrath.

At 9 A.M., the Brethren assembled at the Covered Bridge "to receive the Groundhog prognostication from the Observation Squads." From there it was broadcast to the world. A copious luncheon was enjoyed, and the afternoon was devoted to "fun and frolic at the expense of the Babies

Members of the Slumbering Groundhog Lodge await Orphie's appearance in the 1940s. JAMES E. PENNINGTON COLLECTION

The Lodge inducting Pennsylvania governor William W. Scranton into membership. JAMES E. PENNINGTON COLLECTION

seeking and finding the enlightenment of Arctomancy." The annual banquet commenced at 6:30 P.M., attended by all the present Slumberers appropriately dressed in nightcaps. The names of "three faithful brothers" who were "called to eternal hibernation" during the past year were read amid proper tokens of mourning.

A large class of Baby Groundhogs (new members) was initiated, and honorary membership with the title of Sky Pilot was conferred on the Rev. Wilbur E. Trexler, pastor of the First Reformed Church of Lancaster. That same year, Gen. Mark W. Clark of the Italian campaign in World War II was given honorary membership. Gen. Dwight Eisenhower had preceded him into membership earlier.

The 1971 festivities ended with a call to meditation through the reading of Herman E. Hoch's 1927 poem, as follows:

> Since first a Groundhog had a tail
> One sign was never known to fail
> From prehistoric times till now.

To one great truth all humans bow
The truth is this—no birds will sing
Nor flowers appear of early Spring
When e'er it happily comes to pass
The Groundhog sees on Candlemas
His shadow on the ground.
Why this should be, we do not know
Except, that gods have willed it so.
Would'st thou be wise? By truth abide
Take all the gifts the gods provide
With reverence profound.

Three decades later, the Slumbering Groundhog Lodge is still going strong. The Quarryville festivities are attended by 400 or more devotees, who join approximately 150 Lodge members in enjoying the day. The locus of the event is the White Rock Covered Bridge, south of Quarryville on the west bank of the Octoraro Creek in Colerain Township, Lancaster County. The resident Groundhog—actually a stuffed example fifty years old—is named Octoraro Orphie. Orphie is the principal Pennsylvania rival and competitor of Punxsutawney Phil, and words have been exchanged through the years between the two Groundhog groups, Quarryville calling Phil commercial and Punxsutawney labeling Orphie an upstart. In most years, however, Phil and Orphie agree on their prognostication, whether they predict six more weeks of winter or an early spring.

The Lodge is open to men only, and membership includes professionals of the area and local residents in general, with a sprinkling of attendees from Lancaster and elsewhere. A rustic lodge is their headquarters, where the banquets and other indoor festivities take place. Special events include the dunking of a member in the wintry waters of the creek and the dancing of the Groundhog Jig by selected members. One of the excitements of the day is the catching of a live Groundhog by the Babies, which is then let loose along the creek. In 2002, a cross-dressing Miss Orphie contest was held, the winner of which received a rhinestone crown. Thus pop culture is invading the Quarryville event, just as happened at Punxsutawney and wherever Groundhog Day now is celebrated.

Many of the members are senior citizens, who all take it in stride and look forward to partying with their Brother Groundhogs next year. As one of the senior members put it: "It's a tradition around here and a great

Orphie makes his prediction, circa 1985. JAMES E. PENNINGTON COLLECTION

group of guys. We have doctors, businessmen, teachers, the whole cross section. A lot of our members are leaders and doers. They're the people who make things happen. Yet everyone is equal here."

Part of the annual banquet ritual is the Groundhog Creed, a kind of Pledge of Allegiance to the Groundhog and all he stands for, which the men recite in concert:

We believe in the wisdom of the groundhog.

We declare his intelligence to be of a higher order than that of any other animal from the tick of the blackberry to the elephant of the jungle.

We rejoice that he can and does, foretell with absolute accuracy the weather conditions for the six weeks following each second day of February.

We rejoice further that he is magnanimous and permits other hogs, prophets and almanacs to employ their talents on the remaining 46 weeks of each year.

We assert that if he was more of a man and less of a hog he would form a trust and do all the prognosticating, thereby sending Baers, Hicks, Goose Bone and other Hot Air Artists to the woods.

To defend him, his family and his reputation, we pledge ourselves.

To guard him as he slumbers, his habitations, and his haunts, we pledge ourselves.

We welcome him to our clover fields. We bid him dig and delve, invite him to sit on the top rail of our fences to relax and make general survey. We would stay the hand of desperate men who would slay him. We would kill the dog that would excite and ruffle his temper. To defend him with all our might, and at all hazard, we pledge ourselves, our man servants and our maid servants, our oxen, our asses and our assets as a whole.

The Quarryville Slumbering Groundhog Lodge publishes an eight-page program each year, which includes a list of current members, giving each a humorous title, such as Hole Renewal Administrator, Shadow Snooper, Dr. of Arctomys Physics, Slumber Specialist 3rd Class, Progenitor of Prognostication Planning, Weather Forecast Actuary, Guardian Against False Weather Forecasters, Bifocal Shadow Gazer, Superintendent of Mediocre Entertainment, Exalted Groundhog Catcher, and on and on, through reams of amusing trivia, until we reach the end of the list, with an official called the Duke of Dutchification, which appears to be the only reference to anything Pennsylvania Dutch. A list of honorary members includes local congressmen, governors, and state and U.S. senators.

The Quarryville doings rival Punxsutawney's annual festivities. The official Quarryville Slumberers wear top hats with white nightshirts, contrasting with Punxsutawney's black-coat formal garb. The Quarryville banquets, which are featured each year, are like those at Punxsutawney—joyous, even hilarious affairs. In the early years, they were held at the old-fashioned, porticoed Quarryville Hotel, run by the Fritz family. Later, the Lodge held its banquets at various churches.

The
Ninety Fifth
Annual Observance
of

GROUNDHOG DAY

Saturday, February 2, 2002

IN THE 225th YEAR OF THE INDEPENDENCE OF
THE UNITED STATES OF AMERICA

BY

The Slumbering Groundhog Lodge

OF SOUTHERN LANCASTER COUNTY

Likewise in the State of Pennsylvania and the United States of America

Board of Hibernating Governors

James E. Pennington, Chairman

Lord of the Feast - Thomas Regan

Gerald Dunkel	James R. Groff	Charlie Hart
Richard M. Rankin		Robert Ross
Jay F. Newswanger	Paul C. Girvin	Robert Shoemaker

Wendell B. Singles .... Defender of the Faith Emeritas
Stuart J. Mylin .... Defender of the Faith
Jay Hastings .... Non-Corresponding Secretary
Elvin Herr .... Bondless Treasurer
Jack Ferguson .... Sky Pilot

A program for the Slumbering Groundhog Lodge's observance of Groundhog Day. SLUMBERING GROUND-HOG LODGE

Lodge members in their nightshirts and top hats ham it up as Quarryville's Groundhog Day Orchestra. DOUGLAS WITHERS GROFF COLLECTION

James E. Pennington, the current Chairman of the Board of Hibernating Governors, passes on the Groundhog Day tradition to his grandchildren. JAMES E. PENNINGTON COLLECTION

For those who wish to read further on the long history of the Quarryville Lodge, refer to the compendium of Lodge history by member Douglas Withers Groff, *The Slumbering Groundhog Lodge of Quarryville, Pennsylvania, in the 20th Century.* Organized in the form of annals, this huge, impressive tome of 690 pages chronicles the activities of the Lodge from year to year, beginning with 1908 and ending with 2000, when the book was issued. Featured are numerous dated newspaper clippings detailing the Lodge's activities through the years, and community reactions to its annual events, with an occasional snide but good-humored poke at Punxsutawney and its reputation. The book is copiously illustrated with annual programs, photographs of Lodge events, and members' portraits. Among the portraits is one of Douglas Groff, who tells the reader that he has followed in the pawprints of both his grandfather and father as a full-fledged Slumbering Groundhog. While the book was compiled by Groff, many Brother Groundhogs furnished material and reminiscences. Particularly important was the collection of Lodge memorabilia furnished by Dr. James E. Pennington of New Providence, the present leader.

Groundhog Day in Other Pennsylvania Regions

Groundhog Day is observed in other areas of Pennsylvania as well. The following are some stories from the Anthracite Region of Northeastern Pennsylvania, the Sinnamahoning Valley in North-Central Pennsylvania, and Bucks County in Southeastern Pennsylvania.

Anthracite Region

The Pennsylvania Dutch Country in many northeastern counties of the commonwealth overlaps with the Anthracite Region, where, in the heyday of the mining industry, much of America's anthracite was produced. The Pennsylvania Dutch were the first settlers in many areas of the Upper Susquehanna Valley, joined early by New England Yankees and other Anglo-American settlers in the Wilkes-Barre (Wyoming Valley) area. Throughout the nineteenth and early twentieth centuries, these groups were joined by later emigrant groups from Central, Eastern, and Southern Europe—Poles, Russians, Ukrainians, and others, with additional English and Welsh settlers from the British Isles. These all added their churches and social institutions to the mixture, producing a fascinating hybrid culture with many diverse ethnic strands.

George Korson (1899–1967), America's leading industrial folklorist, was a native of the Schuylkill County Anthracite Region. Encouraged by Edith Patterson, librarian of the Pottsville Free Library, he went on to study formally the culture of the region. He began with folksongs and compiled two books with intriguing titles: *Minstrels of the Mine Patch* and *Coal Dust on the Fiddle.* His last book, *Black Rock: Mining Folklore of the Pennsylvania Dutch,* published in 1960, includes about four pages on Groundhog Day. J. Hampton Haldeman, pharmacist of Pine Grove, Schuylkill County, whom Korson referred to as a local authority on Groundhog Day, reminisced about the custom and the day as they talked in the back room of his drugstore:

> Groundhog is the common English name; *Grundsow* is the Pennsylvania Dutch name; but woodchuck is the true, official name. The only name for the critter is woodchuck. February the second, this animal which has been hibernating for the past several months, comes out of a hole in the ground, and looks around. If it sees its shadow it immediately turns back into its abode, meaning that we're going to have six more weeks of winter. For many years I've been studying this honest American animal, and it's never failed yet.

How did I first become interested? Well, this is a true story what [sic] I'm going to relate. I'm going to go back about fifty years. At that time I heard my father discussing politics and other matters with a companion, and later he mentioned about tomorrow being Groundhog Day.

I was only a child then, but I decided to play hookey from school the following morning, and watch this groundhog. I got up real early and, to my amazement, I discovered a groundhog coming out of the hole about a quarter to eight.

I made the terrible mistake of returning home before eleven o'clock; school left out at eleven. I came home at ten. My father asked why I was home so early from school. I informed him that I went to look for the groundhog. My dad did not lick me. He did not scold me. He merely asked me, "Did you see the groundhog?" I said, "Yes, I did." He inquired, "Did it see its shadow?" I told him, "Yes, it did."

And I also predicted at that time that we were going to have a blizzard. Well, I was in a sweat for several weeks, but we got our blizzard.

Ever since then I've been predicting the weather on February the second. I'm not crowing or bragging, but my score has been one hundred per cent accurate.

The Sinnamahoning Valley

The lumbering days in the pine woods of North-Central Pennsylvania, when the creeks and rivers were full of rafts taking the timber downstream to Lock Haven and Williamsport, were thrilling times. The timbermen worked in the woods cutting the trees in the winter and were dependent on the weather to get their logs to market. A charming book of reminiscences by George William Huntley Jr., entitled *A Story of the Sinnamahone* (1936), gives many details of the primitive life and work patterns in the valley of the Sinnamahoning River, a fifty-mile-long stream that joins the West Branch of the Susquehanna River at Keating in Clinton County. The lumbermen who worked the woods after the Civil War were a mixed crowd. There were Pennsylvania Dutchmen, natives of the area or from other counties; various other Pennsylvanians; a large number of Down-Easters from Maine; and assorted Canadians from Ontario, Quebec, and the Maritime Provinces. So they had different ways of predicting the weather. Huntley tells of two winters in the 1870s:

> The [first] winter was so cold that the creek was frozen solid, and in many places they left the road and hauled the spars down the creek on the ice. . . .
> This unusually hard winter was followed by an unusually mild winter. The

following December, January, and February were warm and smokey. On Candlemas Day there was a general rain and fog. The groundhog came out and got soaking wet but it did not see its shadow. Uncle Elias Foster, who was the Nestor of the East Fork weather fraternity, had been watching the caterpillar for signs and predicted there would be no winter. Dutchie Sibert, of goose-bone fame, said the goose-bone indicated there would be no winter. The proverbial six weeks, allowed for the groundhog to hibernate, had expired and everybody believed spring had come to stay, when suddenly, on St. Patrick's Day, a cold wave appeared, followed by a heavy blanket of snow and then four successive weeks at near zero weather. Everybody got their timber in, after having bewailed the calamity they would suffer by reason of their timber not getting to market.

Bucks County

In the year 2000 in Bucks County in the country outside Doylestown, the county seat, a group of enthusiastic first-timers consulted a local groundhog named Progress Patty and her daughter Peppermint. Three hours after Punxsutawney Phil had seen his shadow and issued his prognostication of six more weeks of winter, Patty delivered her prediction, as reported by the Levittown *Courier-Times*.

> Alas, alack and woe is me,
> My shadow do I see.
> The days ahead are dark and drear,
> Six weeks of winter do I fear!

Daughter Peppermint, actually a Beanie Baby hedgehog, joined Mother Patty, and the attendees broke out into song:

> Boo hoo hoo, we're so blue!
> Here on Progress when shadows come,
> Six more weeks till we have sun!

Then all the celebrants headed for a neighboring home for coffee, pastries, and warmth.

The Bucks County celebration is the brainchild of Peggy George, who on her walks through the neighborhood noticed numerous groundhog holes punctuating the hillsides and fields, and decided to invite her neighbors to a Groundhog Day event. The impromptu verses recited on the occasion already show the shaping up of a ritual to be repeated in years to come.

Groundhog Day Outside of Pennsylvania

The spread of Groundhog Day lore and custom outside the borders of Pennsylvania, the home country of the Pennsylvania Dutch, who introduced it all to America, was accomplished in two ways: As Pennsylvanians migrated outside the state, selected aspects of Pennsylvania Dutch folk culture, including Groundhog lore, were spread to many areas of the United States and Canada. More recently, the twentieth-century commercialization of Groundhog Day helped transform the Groundhog and his day from folk belief to popular-culture icon.

The migration of Pennsylvanians, including thousands of Pennsylvania Dutchmen, began before the Revolution with settlers heading southward to Maryland, Virginia, and the Carolinas. After the Revolution, there was a significant movement northward to the Genesee Country of New York, the adjoining parts of Ontario, and New Brunswick. During the entire nineteenth century, Pennsylvanians were on the move westward, into many counties of the Midwest as well as the trans-Mississippi areas of Iowa, Missouri, Kansas, and Nebraska. This significant movement of population planted Pennsylvania Dutch culture in all the new settlements. Included were farming techniques, farmhouse and barn architecture, preindustrial technology and craftsmanship, foodways, speech patterns, and religion. In the mix was a hefty folkloric component involving proverbial lore, folktales, jests, and weather lore, including the whole Groundhog Day phenomenon. It is quite possible that in some states, such as Wisconsin, Illinois, and Texas, the February 2 lore, which is European in origin, while planted first by the Pennsylvania Dutch, was seconded and thus strengthened by the thousands of German immigrants who arrived in America after the Napoleonic Wars.

Maryland

The folklore of Maryland is closely related to that of Pennsylvania. For Pennsylvania Dutch lore, this is particularly true of the Frederick and Hagerstown areas in Western Maryland. Volume 18 of the series *Memoirs of the American Folklore Society* is a 1925 book entitled *Folk-Lore from Maryland, Collected by Annie Weston Whitney and Caroline Canfield Bullock*. Candlemas Day, February 2, the authors say, "is better known in Maryland as 'Groundhog Day.'" On that day, the Groundhog, "waking from his long slumber, stretches himself and comes out of his hole to look for his shadow." If he sees it, "he hurries back into his hole, to remain in the hole during the forty rainy days that will follow." Maryland is slightly more southern than Pennsylvania, hence rain rather than severe winter weather is predicted. In other items recorded in Maryland, *seven* more weeks of winter are indicated if the Groundhog sees his shadow. And finally, there is this strange bit of lore: "It is very unlucky to keep Christmas greens hanging after Groundhog Day or Candlemas Day."

The Shenandoah Valley

In the Shenandoah Valley of Virginia, where Pennsylvanians settled early in the eighteenth century, Groundhog Day lore was collected by Elmer Lewis Smith, John G. Stewart, and M. Ellsworth Kyger and published in 1964 in *The Pennsylvania Germans of the Shenandoah Valley*. They found that the Pennsylvania Dutch of the region "look for the groundhog on Candlemas, for it is claimed that if he comes out on that day and sees his own shadow, there will be six more weeks of winter weather." The authors quote a ninety-two year old woman: "Folks used to say that the groundhog ruled the weather."

Among the Amish

Pennsylvania's Amish population has expanded into twenty states, seeking new land for agricultural settlement, and it is still expanding into new areas in the twenty-first century. The Old Order Amish, who pride themselves on rejecting certain aspects of common Pennsylvania Dutch folk culture, like the Christmas tree and the Easter rabbit, nevertheless accord at least some recognition to the Groundhog lore of weather prophecy on Candlemas. The national Amish newspaper, the *Budget*, published in Ohio since 1892, provides plentiful evidence that the Amish in various sections of the country observe the Groundhog lore. The columns of each issue of the *Budget* include lengthy and detailed reports from the different Amish settlements, sent in by local people called "scribes" in nineteenth-century newspaper terminology. These report on personalia (deaths, births, weddings, and moves), the weather, and the state of the crops. As reported in Elmer S. Yoder's 1990 volume *I Saw It in the Budget*, in February, scribes often mention the Groundhog.

Groundhog Rivals

Weather-prognosticating Groundhogs have been appearing outside Pennsylvania's borders in recent years. Here is a list of some of the more famous ones in the United States and Canada.

Arkla-homa Will	Arkansas
Balzac Billie	Balzac, Alberta
Birmingham Bill	Birmingham, Alabama
Buckeye Chuck	Marion, Ohio
Chester	St. Louis, Missouri
Chilly Charlie	Woodstock, Ontario
Chuck Wood	Los Angeles, California
Connecticut Chuckles	Manchester, Connecticut
Dixie Dan	Tupelo, Mississippi
Dunkirk Dave	Dunkirk, New York
Florida Phyllis	Apopka, Florida
French Creek Freddie	French Creek, West Virginia
Gen. Beauregard Lee	Lilburn, Georgia
Holland Huckleberry	Holland, Ohio
Jimmy	Sun Prairie, Wisconsin
Metompkin Max	Metompkin, Virginia
Noah, the One-Eyed Groundhog*	Oxford, Michigan
Pee Wee	Mile Square Farm, Vermont
Pennichuck Chuck	Hollis, New Hampshire
Pierre C. Shadeaux	New Iberia, Louisiana
Ridge Lea Larry	Buffalo, New York
Shubenacadie Sam	Nova Scotia
Sir Walter Wally	Raleigh, North Carolina

A scribe called "Cricket," whose report from Glasco, Kansas, was published on February 14, 1895, writes, "Someone should have loaned the Groundhog an umbrella; but it seemed that everybody was afraid and we will have to stand about six weeks more of winter." In the February 15, 1900, issue, Levi J. Lee of Arthur, Illinois, writes, "The groundhog will surely see his shadow today; according to the old saying, there will be six weeks solid winter yet." A somewhat skeptical octogenarian from Berlin, Ohio, M.

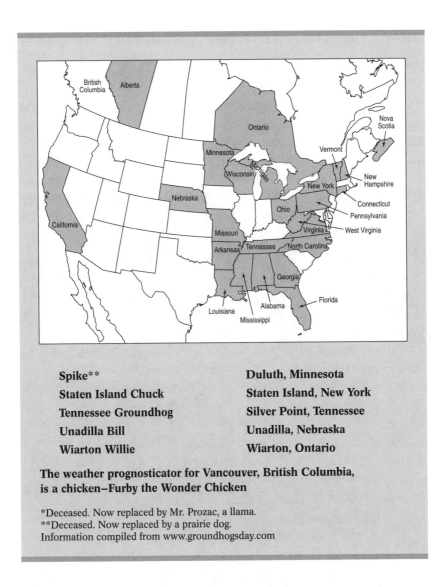

Spike**	Duluth, Minnesota
Staten Island Chuck	Staten Island, New York
Tennessee Groundhog	Silver Point, Tennessee
Unadilla Bill	Unadilla, Nebraska
Wiarton Willie	Wiarton, Ontario

The weather prognosticator for Vancouver, British Columbia, is a chicken–Furby the Wonder Chicken

*Deceased. Now replaced by Mr. Prozac, a llama.
**Deceased. Now replaced by a prairie dog.
Information compiled from www.groundhogsday.com

J. Miller, writing in the February 7, 1912, issue, makes the comment, "Well the groundhog saw his shadow, and now we will have six more weeks of cold weather. I have lived 85 years and I can not tell whether this saying is true or not." In the February 13, 1941, issue, Mrs. Alvin Kropf, writes from Harrisburg, Oregon: "The groundhog could see his shadow very plainly on Sunday if there were any groundhogs here, which there aren't, anyway the old ruse about having six weeks of winter isn't very reliable in Oregon."

Jimmy the Sun Prairie Groundhog of Wisconsin

For more than fifty years, the members of the Sun Prairie, Wisconsin, Groundhog Club have been proclaiming their town to be the World Headquarters of the Groundhog, and the Groundhog Capital of the World. Sun Prairie's congressman one year made bold to declare that Sun Prairie groundhogs are "legitimate and that those in Pennsylvania were otherwise." This led immediately to a response from Punxsutawney's

Jimmy the Groundhog of Sun Prairie, Wisconsin, prepares to prognosticate.
SUN PRAIRIE CHAMBER OF COMMERCE

congressman, and both diatribes were duly published in the *Congressional Record.*

The Sun Prairie weather-predicting Groundhog is called Jimmy. Through the winsome cartoons of Katie Grogan Hoeppner, Jimmy has become beloved as the "Spokes-Hog" for Sun Prairie events. Hoeppner has been producing these tidbits of friendly humor since 1986.

When Jimmy emerged from his burrow about 7 A.M. on the foggy morning of February 2, 2003, his fan club cheered his arrival. Mayor Orfan welcomed Jimmy and, leaning close to him, heard the Groundhog say, "I can't see a thing today!–Early Spring!"

The town goes all out on Jimmy's Day each year. Attractive Groundhog greeting cards, designed by Katie Hoeppner, wish the recipients a "Happy Groundhog Day." Chocolate Groundhogs are available from a local confectioner. The proceedings with Jimmy are broadcast live on February 2, from 6:30 to 10 A.M. Persons with birthdays on Groundhog Day are given special certificates by the town authorities.

Buckeye Chuck, Ohio's Weather Rodent

Punxsutawney Phil's chief competitor in the state of Ohio is Buckeye Chuck, the Weather Rodent of Marion in Central Ohio. According to Chuck's historian, Neil Zurcher, in his attractive book *Ohio Oddities* (2001), Groundhog Day at Marion was initiated years ago by Charley Evers of radio station WMRN of Marion.

The first few years of the celebration, Chuck failed to leave his burrow on February 2, despite all the TV cameras focused on his hole. To satisfy the media reporters, the following year the town fathers borrowed a somewhat nasty Groundhog from a local trapper; fortunately no one was bitten when he was released from his cage. Next year a stuffed Groundhog was featured, to the boos of the big-city media. Evers finally made contact with the state wildlife agency in Columbus and borrowed a cute, little tame Groundhog, and this has been the tradition ever since. Buckeye Chuck poses for the cameras, squeaks into the microphones, and then returns to Columbus by car to slumber the rest of the winter away.

With the growing publicity accorded to Marion's Groundhog, the city's state representative finally sponsored a bill in the state legislature naming Buckeye Chuck Ohio's official Groundhog.

General Beauregard Lee, Georgia's Official Prognosticator

Georgia's charming ex-Confederate Groundhog, General Beauregard Lee, adds a Deep South touch to the national Groundhog Day celebration. At the Yellow River Game Ranch in Lilburn, Georgia, Groundhog Beau, as he is generally called, leaves his white-columned mansion at sunrise on February 2. Encouraged by crowds of Beau Boosters filling the bleachers shouting, "Go, Beau!" the General makes his annual prophecy.

On Groundhog Day 2003, the twenty-third annual event at Lilburn, thirteen-year-old Beau was awakened by Gwinnett County commissioner John Dunn, ringing an old-fashioned farm bell. Beau did not see his shadow and predicted an early spring. Here are some amusing details of the event, from the press release, titled "Beau to Prophesy Weather and Meaning of Life":

> General Beau Lee, Ph.D., Georgia's Official Weather Prognosticator, will perform his annual shadow seeking duty, even though the holiday is on Sunday, February 2nd, 2003 at sunrise. Adding to the suspense is Beau's

Promotional postcard for General Beauregard Lee, Georgia's weather prognosticator. YELLOW RIVER GAME RANCH

adolescent age of thirteen and probably moodiness at being awakened on a wintry weekend. He might prefer southern gospel music on his head set in his bedroom.

To encourage the hundreds of visitors, the Waffle House management will provide "Scattered, Smothered and Covered Hash Browns" in Beau's Bowl. The bleachers crowded with Beau Boosters will be provided with pom-poms and cheer sheets for those who have difficulty remembering, "Go Beau," "Go Beau," "Go Beau."

Architecturally designed swinging doors have been added to Beau's Weathering Heights Mansion. This will contribute to the visual impression of Beau's emergence—nose first, and accommodate his waddling form—should he decide to emerge. Creative landscaping by Pike Nursery will further adorn Beau's lavish Weathering Heights Plantation.

The Honorable Sonny Perdue, newly elected Governor of Georgia, has issued a Proclamation, which "recognizes Beau as 'Georgia's Official Weather Prognosticator,' and further pays special tribute to him for his precise, annual prediction which enables Southerners to effectively prepare for the coming season."

And this is the way they put the weather prediction in Georgia:

If Beau spies his pudgy image, at least six more weeks of winter will occur. Should Beau not find his shadow, citizens may anticipate spring and allergies in six weeks. Last year's announcement was again correct when Beau predicted an early spring. By February 23rd, green buds had appeared on willow trees. On March 16th, the last day of the six week prediction period, sunbathers enjoyed a balmy 78 degrees. Beau has an extraordinary 99% rate of accuracy.

The Yellow River Game Ranch, venue of Georgia's annual Groundhog Day festivities, is the oldest animal preserve in the state. For forty-one years, it has been introducing people-friendly wildlife to children and adults.

Groundhog Day Misfires in Texas

In a 1989 article published in *Antiques and Auction News*, well illustrated with Groundhog Lodge program covers, treated as collectibles by the author, Leon Thompson furnishes some amusing reminiscences of his boyhood days in Texas:

One of the strangest celebrations I knew of was in my childhood days in the old oil boom town of Wink, Texas. During the Depression, when times were tough everywhere, oil gave the "boomtowners" an edge on living it up when they celebrated Groundhog Day. Few, if any, knew just what a groundhog looked like out there in the prairie, but with all of the cowboys from the nearby ranches and the oilfield roughnecks lifting their drinks to "toast" the groundhog, no one cared what it looked like.

I'll always remember my last Groundhog Day celebration, in about 1937. As a child, I kept out of the way, but I enjoyed the "highlights" of the special celebration that year. The mayor of Wink, Texas, was hit with the largest cow chip in Texas . . . some say it was an accident; others do not think it was. It ruined the mayor's ten gallon hat, knocked off the hairpiece no one knew he wore, and quite ruined the mayor's day!

The town's festivities included contests, such as a dexterity competition involving tossing cow chips behind the Oasis Saloon and a footrace in which the saloon waiters from all over town competed. There was a parade, too, with western bands from several saloons furnishing the music. The saloons emptied, and everyone headed for city hall, where the mayor, despite his discomfiture, gave a much appreciated speech. This, however, was interrupted by loud popping sounds, caused by the explosion of a handful of twenty-two bullets that someone had dumped into the iron stove in the mayor's office. The speech ended with the crowd scattering in all directions. It was said later that the sound was produced by "the groundhog chewing on the ten gallon hat which the mayor had left in the office." Thompson relates:

Some also recall that, during the speech, two of the women got into a hair pulling fight. The mayor broke it up by getting between the two ladies, but he sported the biggest black eye you ever saw for days afterward. With a ten gallon hat ruined by a cow chip, his hairpiece smelling like a bull, and the black eye, the mayor dropped the final curtain on Groundhog Day!

CHAPTER III

The Origins of Groundhog Day

The Pennsylvania Dutch culture is an essentially Protestant culture. There were several small rural Roman Catholic settlements in the Colonial period, such as Bally (Goshenhoppen) and Conewago, and a few early churches in cities like Philadelphia, Lancaster, and York, with scattered Catholic families elsewhere through the countryside. But the great majority of the Pennsylvania Dutch population was Protestant: 75 percent "Church Dutch," consisting of Lutheran and Reformed, and 25 percent "Sectarian Dutch," including Mennonites, Amish, Brethren, and other small groups. The now archaic Pennsylvania High German language that was used in the nineteenth century had terms for these two groups: *Kirchenleute*, or "Church People," and *Sektenleute* or "Sect People."

These groups represented the official Protestant religion of the Pennsylvania Dutch. There was also a *folk* religion, meaning a people's additional or alternative ideas about religion that either go beyond or are opposed to the official theological teachings of the churches. As Dr. Alfred L. Shoemaker, eminent folklife scholar and organizer of the Pennsylvania Dutch Folk Festival at Kutztown, put it, the *official* religion of the Pennsylvania Dutch—the religion of the church organizations—was Protestant, but the *folk* religion was Catholic, meaning it was pre-Protestant or medieval in character. Some of the additional ideas held by many Pennsylvania Dutch, such as the belief in the transfer of evil from a witch to another person through supernatural means and the curious Pennsylvania Dutch system of folk healing known as "powwowing," were often opposed by the clergy, although sometimes only half-heartedly, since witchcraft and curious alternative forms of therapy are certainly represented in the Bible.

In the world of official Protestantism, the high holidays for the church year were the biblical festivals of Christmas, Easter, and Pentecost. The Protestant Reformers had vetoed the medieval cult of the saints, each of which had been assigned special attributes and special days in the calendar year. The people, however, retained in their folk religion some of these medieval saints and remembered some of the folklore associated with their days. February 2 was traditionally the date of Candlemas, a high church festival dedicated to the Virgin Mary.

The Protestant stage of the Pennsylvania Dutch folk religion is about five centuries old, beginning with the Reformation in the opening years of the sixteenth century. The medieval Catholic stage, from which the Protestant stage inherited many potent ideas, preceded that. Even farther back in the past was the Hellenistic era, with its Greek and Roman cultural expressions, whose roots were in Egypt, Palestine, Chaldea, and other parts of the ancient Near East. Some major features of the calendar, including the signs of the zodiac and the astrological approach to the universe, had their origins in this period.

But the roots of Groundhog Day go back still farther than Mediterranean Hellenism. It was the Germanic peoples who gave their language and culture to the Northern and Central European homelands of the ancestors of the Pennsylvania Dutch—Germany, Switzerland, Austria, and Alsace-Lorraine—as well as to Holland, parts of Belgium, and England, the latter through the Anglo-Saxon invasions in the fifth century A.D. Even farther back in the European past than the Germanic invasions, in the prehistoric centuries B.C., the Celtic world and culture predominated in Western Europe. The Celts were a mixture of peoples, related in culture and language, who gave their language to Ireland, Scotland, Wales, Cornwall, and Brittany. Celtic place names are scattered all over the map of Western Europe and the British Isles. Historical geographers and linguists have identified thousands of European river, mountain, valley, and even town names as Celtic in origin.

The Celtic culture had a profound influence on the calendar of Europe, and through migration, this Celtic sense of time has influenced the European colonies of America. The Celts organized their year into four major seasons: winter, or the dark half of the year, divided into first half and second half, and summer, the light half of the year, divided in the same way. The seasonal turning points in the Celtic year were immensely important communal festivals in prehistoric, pre-Christian times. Of these festivals, the dates have continued to be important down to the present time, though the celebrations were transformed by the medieval Church into "Christian" holidays. The four turning points of the Celtic year were November 1, February 1, May 1, and August 1. The year began with November 1, the Celtic New Year, and ended with the Harvest Festival of August 1. The Celtic names for the four festivals were *Samhain, Imbolc, Beltaine*, and *Lughnasa*.

All of these transitional days looked to the future, looked ahead to the next season, the coming three-month period, and hence were weather-important days. All of them also were sun festivals and fire festivals, with festive fires lighted on the hills and fire rituals performed, such as driving cattle between two fires to protect them for the coming season. Fires were symbolic of the all-important, life-giving sun, which ruled in the heavens and on which our primitive fur-clad European ancestors were dependent for their very lives. In some areas of the Celtic world, wheels were lighted with burning straw and rolled down the hills to symbolize the transit of the sun and magically help it grow in power from the dark half of the year (winter) to the light half (summer).

For the ancient Europeans, these days were so crucial and so embedded in their cultural sense of time that when the Western European peoples were Christianized, the new Church, unable to root them out, "baptized" them into Christian holidays. May 1 became May Day, originally associated with the Virgin Mary and later a secular spring festival, with maypole, May queen, and other folkloric customs. August 1 became in Britain *Lammas*, or "Loaf-Mass Day," when the farmers' wives brought the first loaves of bread baked from the new harvest of grain to the church to be blessed. Since November 1 in the Celtic year was a day devoted to the dead, the Church made it into All Saints' Day. But the people continued to celebrate the eve of the old holiday as Halloween, with its many harmless folkloric customs that have come all the way down to our day. February 1, extended into February 2, became Candlemas, and eventually Groundhog Day.

Why Predict the Weather?

The pioneer Pennsylvania farmer, whether Pennsylvania Dutch or not, like all early American dwellers on the land and tillers of the soil, faced a constant struggle to make his livelihood and support a growing family. Like other rural groups, the Pennsylvania Dutch produced large families. Their children helped out with the farm and household work, assisting their parents and thus learning by unofficial apprenticeship the arts of agriculture, gardening, and household management. Complicating the economic picture for the father was the fact that his sons had to be provided with help when they grew up, married, and started farming. The custom was for the father to help the sons get settled on a farm, while the daughters were provided for by their husbands and husbands' families. In some cases, when the youngest son married, the parental farm was turned over to him and the parents stayed on, "retired" but not really retired, living in a separate house called the *Grossdawdy*, or "Grandfather," House. This is still the custom among the Old Order Amish.

The Pennsylvania farm folk, making a living from the soil, had a different relationship to the environment than we do today. Whatever their religious orientation, they did not see the earth as nature, or Mother Nature's

Farmers needed ways to forecast the weather, as they were dependent on their harvests. ROUGHWOOD COLLECTION

Father Winter in the midst of an agricultural society. ROUGHWOOD COLLECTION

realm, but rather as creation, the gift of the Creator to mankind to use and take care of as good stewards, to use a favorite Protestant word. But while the earth and the soil were a divine gift to mankind, our ancestors were dependent on the weather. Heavy snows and ice storms in the winter or early spring could damage growing crops and provide difficult times. Excessive summer heat combined with a long dry spell could endanger the expected and needed harvest.

Hence the pioneer farm families turned to various traditional means of attempting to predict the weather. This prediction system could be very elaborate. The calendar provided the basic, underlying time framework for their lives. Every farmhouse had a printed calendar called an *almanac*, a booklet that customarily hung on a hook in the kitchen, where it was frequently consulted for the "up signs" and "down signs" of the moon, as well as the influence of the signs of the zodiac on the earth and on individual lives. This was an ancient system of organizing the planets and constellations in the heavens into an understandable pattern that was believed to show how the heavens influenced both the earth and mankind. For centuries, our European and American farmer ancestors took these ideas seriously, believing them as part of their worldview, as adjuncts to or even integral parts of their religious faith. Our ancestors thus believed in the unity of the universe and drew connections between heaven and earth, and mankind and the earth, including the use of plants for nourishment and healing. And finally, mankind and the animal world were seen as connected and interacting with each other in God's creation.

Our ancestors were geared into the universe and linked with the natural environment in ways that we today have either completely forgotten or no longer fully accept. The environment-friendly movements of the present day are in part a truncated substitute for this earlier folk universe. But most of them provide scientific, rational attitudes to our natural surroundings, without the traditional lore of linking man to the heavens through the zodiac and other beliefs now considered irrational and folkloristic.

The Calendar and the Almanac

Understanding how our farming forefathers, whether peasants in Europe, yeoman farmers in the British Isles, or Pennsylvania farmers in the New World, viewed the weather and attempted to predict it requires a close look at the calendar. In their folk-cultural world, there were two frameworks involving time. The first involved rites of passage, which marked the rituals and social changes in an individual's life, from birth, through puberty, courtship, and marriage, to death and burial. The second is the calendric year, with customs assigned to specific days and seasons, either agricultural, with the progression through the seasons and the work and customs associated with each period, or ecclesiastical, marking the religious year as it proceeds from festival to festival. In European as well as early American folk culture, these frameworks were combined, and the days and seasons were viewed as the farmer's time system, alternating work with leisure, everydayness with festive celebration. Today most of us no longer work at home as our farmer forefathers did, and we celebrate only a minimal calendar of favorite holidays, most of them rife with commercialism.

Adler Calender
*for the year 1900,
Reading, Pennsyl-
vania.* ROUGHWOOD
COLLECTION

The Philadelphia presses issued English almanacs as early as the 1690s. The Germantown printer Christopher Sauer (Sower) Sr. (1693–1758) issued the first successful German almanac, *Der Hoch-Deutsche Amerikanische Calender,* or "High German American Almanac," in 1738. The English-language almanacs included Benjamin Franklin's *Poor Richard's Almanac,* which became a vehicle of humor and popular literature. Most of us can still quote some of Franklin's clever aphorisms, such as "A penny saved is a penny earned" and "Early to bed and early to rise, makes a man healthy, wealthy, and wise." But all the almanacs attempted to predict the weather, mostly through astrological guesswork, without computers, satellites, and all the other accoutrements of current meteorology, of course.

In addition to its focus on the calendar and the weather, the yearly almanac became a vehicle of popular instruction, providing articles on gardening, medicine, and other household hints. Christopher Sauer Jr. (1721–84) published in his almanac, in serial installations from 1762 to 1778, his *Kurzgefasstes Kräuterbuch,* or "Concise Herbal," which gave information on 266 plants, including their medical and culinary uses. In addition to his printing business, Sauer ran an apothecary shop and supplied herbs for it from his extensive Germantown garden. His *Kräuterbuch* was the first herbal printed in America and was intended to be kept and sewn together as a useful household handbook. The entire book has been translated and edited by food historian William Woys Weaver as *Sauer's Herbal Cures: America's First Book of Botanic Healing, 1762–1778*.

From the very beginning, the yearly almanac also was looked forward to–and kept–as a source of humor, jests, short stories, descriptions of animals (including monsters), and remarkable accidents, such as steamboat explosions in the nineteenth century, complete with exciting or gruesome woodcut illustrations. Almanacs were popular, and occasionally at country sales, bushel baskets full of old almanacs have been brought down from the farmhouse attic and auctioned off, appropriately covered with fly specks from their long stay under the house-roof.

One of the best introductions on how the almanac worked in the Pennsylvania Dutch folk culture is the series of articles published in *Pennsylvania Folklife* from 1972 to 1975, "Pennsylvania German Astronomy and Astrology," from the pen of Professor Louis Winkler of the Department of Astronomy at the Pennsylvania State University. The first issue, focusing on almanacs, has an especially useful section, "How to Read an Almanac." This explains for the lay reader the complicated signs, symbols, and astronomical/astrological information printed in the eight columns on the pages devoted to each particular month in the calendar year. The extracts from the so-called *Hundred Year Calendar* dealing with the weather for the year are also valuable.

In these days of scientific weather prediction, it is puzzling indeed to know how the almanac calculators dared to predict weather for the coming year. One of the most popular almanacs in the Dutch Country in the nineteenth and twentieth centuries was the Hagerstown *Town and Country Almanac*, begun by printer John Gruber in 1797. The cover of the Bicentennial Issue of 1976 announces, among other things, that the pages within include "Best Days for Planting, Weeding, Harvesting," "Hints for the Housewife and Handyman," and "Conjecture of the Weather and Other Astronomical Facts."

To sample the weather prognostications of a Pennsylvania almanac and attempt to understand how the almanac calculators predicted the weather, let's look at the German almanac *Der Neue Reading Adler Calender* for 1898, published by Berks County's oldest newspaper, the Reading *Adler*. It appears that most of the calculations were based on lunar astrology. For each month, the days and times when the moon entered each of its quarters were given, with the moon's conjectural influence on the weather. The German has it *"Monds-Viertel mit ihren muthmasslichen Witterungen."* The word *Witterung* means weather, state of the atmosphere, and temperature. The judiciously used word *muthmasslich* means conjectural, presumable, or probable.

On this basis of supposed lunar influences, the almanac's prognostications for January 1898 are as follows: 1–3, mild and windy; 4–5, changeable; 6–8, snow; 9–10, clear; 11–12, south wind; 13–15, rain; 16–18, clear and cold; 19–20, changeable; 21–23, snow; 24–25, cold; 26–27, cloudy; 28–29, windy; and 30–31, changeable. In addition, the 1898 issue provides predictions for the seasons, including the conjectural weather for some specific months, based on the *Hundertjähriger Calender für das Jahr 1898*, or "Hundred-Year Calendar for the Year 1898."

That the Pennsylvania Dutchman of the past often accepted the weather predictions in his almanacs, or at least studied them as he planned his farm work, is borne out by an Episcopalian storekeeper of Morgantown, Berks County, in the 1840s. The diary of James L. Morris, who recorded the lore and practices of his Pennsylvania Dutch neighbors, has for February 1, 1845: "The coldest day of the season so far as we have got into it. And what is a little remarkable the almanacs both German and English prophecied [*sic*] it 'the coldest day of the season.'" This striking coincidence will "have the effect of strengthening the faith of those who put their belief in almanac prognostications. The Germans of our neighborhood do this much more than their English neighbours, indeed with some of the old ones, the purchase of an almanac, or rather the choosing of one, is quite a matter of importance." This reflects the fact that Morgantown was between the circulation areas of the historic Lancaster almanacs and those published in Reading. And of course, the Germantown almanacs circulated among the upcountry Dutch as well.

History of Candlemas

On the medieval Catholic calendar, February 2 was Candlemas, or Candlemas Day. Like most church holidays, this one is complex. Candles, symbolic of the Divine Light, were on that day carried in procession and brought to the churches to be blessed for use in church and home. These candle customs were evidently of pagan origin but were continued in connection with the Christian festival. To Christianize the pagan holiday, the Church added two traditions based on its own belief system. Because February 2 was forty days after December 25, the Church, following the Jewish custom of the purification of women after childbirth, named the day the Feast of the Purification of the Virgin Mary. In German, the day is called *Mariä-Lichtmess,* or "St. Mary's Candle Mass." A second Christian note was struck by connecting the holiday with the Presentation of Jesus in the Temple. According to the Gospel of Luke, the aged prophet Simeon was waiting for this to happen. Taking the child in his arms, he blessed God with thanksgiving for having seen "thy salvation, which thou hast prepared before the face of all people; a light to lighten the Gentiles, and the glory of thy people Israel" (Luke 2:30–32).

According to W. Carew Hazlitt's *Faith and Folklore* (1905), based on Brand's *Popular Antiquities of Great Britain,* the word *purification* "carries in its original meaning the idea of cleansing by fire or light, and hither, rather than perhaps to Jesus Christ being the Spiritual Light, we ought to refer the connection of candles with this festival." The celebration of the Purification of the Virgin on this candle-centered day, however, illustrates the engrafting of Christian significance onto a pagan holiday. Again according to Hazlitt, this was "a piece of questionable clerical diplomacy, since it was apparently inconsistent with [the dogma] of the Immaculate Conception."

Further light is also thrown on the involvement of candles with this calendar day from the fact that the pagan, pre-Christian Romans carried torches and candles in a nightly procession on February 2 to honor their goddess Februa, for whom February was said to have been named. This they did in order to curry her favor to influence her powerful son Mars, for whom March is named, to favor their undertakings. This is essentially the same process as developed in Christianity, where the common believer attempted to curry favor with Mary the Divine Mother, so that she could then influence the almost unapproachable Christ, who as a member of the Trinity was seated at the right hand of God the Father, hence was in on all heavenly decisions.

Thus throughout the Catholic Middle Ages, the candles of Candlemas were in honor of Mary, to gain her favor to influence her son. But the Protestant Church of England gave the day another significance. In 1537, Henry VIII in a proclamation on rites and ceremonies laid down the following ruling: "On Candlemas Daye it shall be declared, that the bearynge of candels is done in the memorie of Christe the spirituall lyghte, whom Simeon dyd prophecye as it is redde in the Churche that daye." This is a reference to the Presentation of Christ in the Temple. As Protestantism continued to expand in England, many groups arose that opposed the Anglican Church's continuation of the Candlemas rites. Indeed, they opposed the Church's continued tolerance of all the traditional medieval Catholic holidays devoted to the Virgin Mary. The Puritans cleansed their temple by forbidding candles in churches and meetinghouses on Candlemas.

During the Middle Ages, folklore grew around the religious festival of Candlemas. In particular, this lore was focused on predicting the weather. Chambers's standard 1863 work, *The Book of Days: A Miscellany of Popular Antiquities in Connection with the Calendar*, contains an extended section on Candlemas that reports much of the folklore about the day from the British Isles. "Considering the importance attached to Candlemass day for so many ages," Chambers writes, "it is scarcely surprising that there is a universal superstition throughout Christendom, that good

February page from the 1900 Adler Calender, *Reading, Pennsylvania.* Lichtmess *is February 2.* ROUGHWOOD COLLECTION

weather on this day indicates a long continuance of winter and a bad crop, and that its being foul is, on the contrary, a good omen."

Chambers quotes a popular Scottish rhyme, recorded in the nineteenth century, that expresses this idea:

> If Candlemass day be dry and fair,
> The half o' winter's to come and mair;
> If Candlemass day be wet and foul,
> The half o' winter's gane at Yule.

The Background of Groundhog Lore

Though the Candlemas lore from the British Isles, brought to America by our English ancestors, dealt with weather prognostication, no groundhog or other animal was involved. But our German forebears also had folklore surrounding Candlemas, and this lore includes an animal and his shadow in conjunction with predicting the weather.

The *Handwörterbuch des Deutschen Aberglaubens*, or the *Dictionary of German Folk Belief*, has an article on *Lichtmess*, or Candlemas. "Above all," it says, "Candlemas is decisive for the weather of the coming time, and with it also for the fruitfulness of the year." This massive encyclopedia reports many sayings, from all parts of German-speaking Europe, about what sort of weather the day predicts if it is bright or dark: "A dark Candlemas brings plentiful food on the table, a bright Candlemas brings want." "If Candlemas is bright and clear, the crops will be damaged and it will be a bad year." "The sun should shine on Candlemas only as long as it takes for a rider to saddle his horse; if longer, expect a late Spring." "If the sun shines on the minister preaching in his pulpit, i.e., if it is a sunny day that lights the whole church, expect a bad year." "If the sun on Candlemas shines on the manure pile, the farmer should lock the fodder in the chest," meaning that fodder will be scarce. These are only a few of the numerous Germanic sayings about Candlemas and its connection with weather prediction, collected in the early twentieth century by the editors.

This European encyclopedia also cites the *Dachs*, or badger, as the Candlemas weather prophet throughout much of German-speaking Europe, although in some areas, a fox or bear was observed. *Dachstag*, or Badger Day, is a German folk expression for Candlemas. The belief was the same as that in Pennsylvania Dutch Groundhog lore–if the badger encountered sunshine on Candlemas and therefore saw his shadow, he crawled back into his hole to stay for four more weeks, which would be a continuation of winter weather. In America, the four weeks became six.

The German badger lives in the woods, and his personality, like that of the Groundhog, is characterized by extreme shyness. He was mentioned by the naturalists of antiquity, Aristotle and Pliny, as well as by medieval writers. In popular usage, badgers were divided, evidently from the shape of their snouts, into two distinct types: "dog badgers" and "pig badgers."

In folk medicine, badger fat was considered nearly a universal healer, and even today, the windows of health stores and apothecary shops in Germany advertise badger fat. In the past, it was applied to the body to heal everything from hernias to goiter, and especially wounds, and it was even considered a practical remedy for *böses Blut*, ill will or ill feeling between friends or neighbors. Parts of the badger's body also were used in healing, its liver and heart in particular. Even an artistically mounted badger's tooth was considered protection against pestilence and against evil effects of the elements, such as hail and storms. Badger paws were used as amulets, placed on animals and children to ward off danger. In certain parts of Germany, a badger skin was hung from the neck of the off horse in a team—the one to the right, away from the wagoner, who sat behind the left, or lead, horse.

With all these medical and protective uses connected with the European cult of the badger, it is strange that when the Pennsylvania Dutch adopted the Groundhog in his place, they did not transfer such qualities to their new American Candlemas weather predictor.

In areas that observed the bear—an animal that, like the badger, also hibernates—if the bear could "see over the mountain," in other words, if the weather was clear on Candlemas, he had to spend six more weeks hibernating in his lair. But if it rained or snowed on Candlemas, the bear demolished his shelter because he was no longer afraid of winter weather. The old children's ditty "The Bear Went over the Mountain" might possibly have some distant connection with this ancient belief. After all, the "bear went over the mountain, to see what he could see!"

In the 1946 *Folk Tale, Fiction and Saga in the Homeric Epics*, the Bryn Mawr scholar Rhys Carpenter points to the bear tradition as the ultimate root of our Groundhog Day. The American Groundhog tradition does not derive from the British Isles, he says, where there is no similar badger lore, but from the Germanic badger tradition, which he postulates grew out of "the still earlier pan-European bear cult, in which the bear features as weather prophet." He continues with this thought:

> Beyond the Slavic radius, in regions where the bear was not so sacrosanct or perhaps had grown so scarce that his dens were no longer to be found (but as far as my information goes, only on German soil), this same superstition was transferred from the bear to the much smaller badger, which is also a hibernant. German immigrants to Pennsylvania brought this tradition with them and, in default of badgers, fixed it on the much more plentiful and very bearlike little marmot, the groundhog, whose modern official name of *Arctomys monax* confirms his bearish properties.

How Old Is Groundhog Day?

How old is Groundhog Day in Pennsylvania? Like the dating of the first Christmas trees in Pennsylvania and the first written notices of our Easter customs, the documentary evidence for Groundhog Day in the local literature does not go back beyond the first half of the nineteenth century.

The earliest evidence found thus far comes from Caernarvon Township in Berks County, Pennsylvania. In the Welsh settlement around Morgantown in that township, a significant proportion of the non-Welsh population was Pennsylvania Dutch, and among these were many Amish settlers. James L. Morris, the Morgantown storekeeper, was of Welsh descent and recorded in his diary numerous bits of folklore that he learned from his Dutch neighbors and customers, whom he refers to as "Germans." Among the weather lore is the following item written on February 2, 1840: "Today the Germans say the groundhog comes out of his winter quarters and if he sees his shadow he returns in and remains there 40 days." This is certainly one of the earliest references to the Groundhog belief associated with Candlemas.

Since Morris in many items compares the recorded situation with remembrances from his own boyhood, the Groundhog lore can likely be pushed back to shortly after the turn of the century, or even into the eighteenth century. No doubt the whole Groundhog mystique developed in eighteenth-century Pennsylvania, when our emigrant ancestors transferred the weather-predicting expertise of the German badger to our native Pennsylvania Groundhog.

CHAPTER IV

Nature's Groundhog

W hat sort of a creature is the Groundhog? Where does he stand in the world of nature? What is his place among the fantastic variety of wild animal species of North America? How has he been described by scientific investigators from the eighteenth to the twenty-first century?

In the nineteenth century, the study of natural objects, including animals, plants, and minerals, was usually subsumed under the umbrella term "natural history." This concept was popular in the schoolbooks of the pre–Civil War era, but today the subjects then covered by this older term are more properly studied separately, under the scientific rubrics of zoology, botany, mineralogy, and other natural sciences.

Out of the wealth of materials that Americans produced concerning natural history in the first half of the nineteenth century, some included analyses of the Groundhog. Two are by at least part-time Pennsylvanians: Richard Harlan and John James Audubon.

Richard Harlan, M.D. (1796–1843), a Quaker naturalist from Chester County, published his groundbreaking volume *Fauna Americana* in 1825. He was a professor of comparative anatomy, surgeon of the Philadelphia Hospital, president of the American Ophthalmic Society, and member of numerous American and European medical and scientific organizations. His other books included *American Herpetology* (1827) and *Medical and*

Physical Researches (1835). In the midst of his scientific career, Dr. Harlan contracted yellow fever in New Orleans, where he died in 1843.

Harlan uses the older taxonomic classification of *Arctomys monax*. Though the animal is called a Groundhog in Pennsylvania, it is known as a woodchuck in Maryland, as well as a Maryland marmot or marmotte du Canada. Harlan's description of the Groundhog is based on "an individual that lived perfectly tame for several months," hence he must have had his own pet Groundhog.

He describes the outward appearance of the animal as "brown above; paler on the sides and under the belly; snout bluish-gray and blackish; tail about half the length of the body, covered with blackish hairs," and fifteen to eighteen inches in total length. The body is clumsy and low set, and the nails are long and sharp, good for digging. The account ends with details on the animal's habits, summarized as follows: The Groundhog "digs deep holes in clover fields, or on the sides of hills, or under rocks in the woods in the neighborhood of fields." The holes usually have several compartments. The animals "feed on herbs and fruits, but delight in clover, of which they destroy immense quantities." When tamed, they are docile, but when attacked out of their holes, "they prefer giving battle to a dog rather than attempt to effect their escape by retreating." In fact, he says, "they are more than a match for a dog a size larger than themselves." They "pass the winter in a state of lethargy," that is, they hibernate.

John James Audubon (1785–1851), the distinguished American naturalist, was a native of Santo Domingo in the West Indies who spent part of his life in Pennsylvania. Audubon the scientist is remembered principally for his contributions to ornithology, with his magnificent plates of North American birds. His equally impressive plates and descriptions of American animal varieties were issued in *The Viviparous Quadrupeds of North America* (1846), in which work he was joined by the Rev. John Bachman, Lutheran minister of Charleston, South Carolina. From this joint project, two immense elephant-folio volumes of color plates were published. Plate no. 2 in volume 1 is entitled "Maryland Marmot–Woodchuck–Groundhog." In it, one young Groundhog is shown in profile with all four feet on the ground. The adult is also in a profile pose but standing up on its two hind feet, resulting in a more animated presence. The other small Groundhog has its teeth bared, giving it a menacing countenance.

Audubon turned his attention fully to documenting North American mammals on his last expedition, which took him up the Missouri River

John James Audubon's Groundhog plate from his 1846 work, The Viviparous Quadrupeds of North America. SPECIAL COLLECTIONS, UNIVERSITY OF PENNSYLVANIA LIBRARY

Valley in 1841 to 1843. There, as his diaries report, he found groundhogs in great numbers living in burrows along the riverbanks. It was on this expedition that he drew the watercolor sketch of three groundhogs, a mother and two young (now in the Morgan Library in New York), on which the plate in his work on American quadrupeds was based. In his diary, he writes that when he showed his finished Groundhog plate to a group of Indians, "one of the women actually ran off at the sight of the Wood Chuck exclaiming that they were alive &c."

Sarah E. Boehme, in her book *John James Audubon in the West: The Last Expedition, Mammals of North America* (2000), considers Audubon's paintings for the woodchuck "important in showing how he would treat the smaller animals." They did not "lend themselves to be seen in the same artistic context as the larger animals; they had no connection with the iconography of the hunt." The smaller mammals were "often less appealing than their ornithological predecessors," yet Audubon managed to imbue his animals with personality.

Like Harlan, Audubon uses the earlier designation of *Arctomys monax*. He mentions in passing that the French Canadians call all marmots *sif-*

fleurs, or "whistlers," because of their habit of whistling to alert their progeny to approaching danger. His description of the Groundhog, based on observation of many specimens, is much the same as that given by Harlan, although more detailed. The average weight of an adult male, he estimates, is nine pounds, eleven ounces. Audubon says that "many individuals of this species seem to prefer stony places, and often burrow close to or in a stone wall." They are, however, not social animals and do not live in communities like their western relatives the prairie dogs. In fact, two Groundhogs are rarely together except when mating or caring for their newborn progeny, which, after several months, they turn loose into the fields to dig their own burrows. He quotes from Godman's *American Natural History* that when feeding in their favorite clover fields, one or more Groundhogs sit erect as sentinels, giving a loud whistle at the approach of danger, "which immediately disperses the troop in every direction, and they speedily take refuge in their deepest caves."

He reports that they "sleep during the greater part of the day, stealing from their burrows early in the morning and towards evening." They sometimes awkwardly climb trees or bushes, and finding a comfortable position

Woodchuck at Home, a photo postcard, circa 1907, by H. E. Rickert of Tower City, Pennsylvania. On the back of the card the persistent photographer informed his correspondent that "it took three weeks, patience and perseverance till I was successful." ROUGHWOOD COLLECTION

in which to sun themselves, they may stay there for hours, reveling in the sunshine. They become fat in the autumn and go into hibernation "about the time the leaves have fallen from the trees" and "the frosty air gives notice of the approach of winter." Each adult remains "burrowed in the earth until the grass has sprung up and the genial warmth of spring invites it to come forth." The hibernation of the Groundhog and other creatures Audubon considered an instance "of the all-wise dispensations of the Creator." He describes hibernation as "this power of escaping the rigours and cold blasts" of winter and "resting securely, in a sleep of insensibility, free from all cravings of hunger and all danger of perishing with cold, till the warm sun of spring, once more calls them into life and activity."

Among the many more contemporary descriptions is an entry in *The Audubon Society Field Guide to North American Mammals*, by John O. Whitaker Jr. et al. (1980), for the woodchuck *(Marmota monax)*, also known as Groundhog or marmot. The animal is described as sun-loving and a good swimmer and climber with a diet of green vegetation. When corn is ripening, it feeds on that, and it "can cause extensive damage in a garden."

Its winter burrow includes a "hibernation chamber where it curls up in a ball on a mat of grass." During hibernation, "body temperature falls from almost 97°F. to less than 40°, breathing slows to once every 6 minutes, and heartbeat drops from over 100 beats per minute to 4."

In early spring, it emerges from hibernation, "according to legend on February 2, 'Groundhog Day,' but much later in northern parts of its range." The male immediately seeks a mate, but "its brief stay in the burrow of a receptive female is almost the only time two adults share a den." The result is a litter of four or five blind young, born in April or May. "The young open their eyes and crawl at about one month," and at two months go out on their own and dig their own holes.

The entry mentions that "woodchuck meat is very good, although eaten by very few." The Groundhog also may benefit the soil.

While an overpopulation can damage cropfields, gardens, and pastures, Woodchucks are beneficial in moderate numbers, for their defecation inside the burrow, in a special excrement chamber separate from the nesting chamber, fertilizes the earth, and their digging loosens and aerates the soil, letting in moisture and organic matter while bringing up subsoil for transformation into topsoil (in New York State, they turn over 1,600,000 tons of soil each year).

Classification and Etymology

The Groundhog has been placed in various scientific classifications of mammals and quadrupeds, some now outmoded. Futhey and Cope's *History of Chester County, Pennsylvania* (1881), in its section on mammalia of the area, lists the Groundhog under the order Rodentia, rodents or gnawing animals, and the subclassification Sciuridae, the squirrel family.

The usual present-day classification of the Groundhog uses the genus term *Marmota*, from which is derived the common name of marmot. This word is from the French *marmotte* and eventually from *marmottaine*, constructed of two Latin words: *mus/muris* and *montanus*, meaning "mountain mouse" or "mountain rodent." The European species, *Marmota marmota*, is found in the higher sections of the Alps and Pyrenees. The American species is today designated *Marmota monax*.

Our Groundhog is found in the northeastern United States and Canada, spreading into the eastern parts of the South (see map). Related species, such as the hoary marmot (*Marmota caligata*) and the yellow-bellied marmot (*Marmota flaviventris*), are found in western North America. The species name *monax* is, curiously, not from the classical languages but, according to American etymologists, from the native Virginian *moonack* or *monack*, meaning, appropriately, "digger."

The most common genus name in earlier scientific classifications, and that used by Harlan and Audubon, was *Arctomys,* a word constructed from the Greek *arktos*, meaning "bear," and *mus/muris*, "mouse or rodent," hence, "bear-mouse" or "bear-rodent." But since *arktos* can also mean "north," as in our English word *arctic*, the combination could also mean "northern rodent."

Woodchuck, the most widespread synonym for Groundhog, familiar to most American children from the tongue-twister "How much wood could a woodchuck chuck if a woodchuck could chuck

Range of the Groundhog in North America.

wood?" is of American Indian origin. It comes, according to etymologists, from *wejack*, a northern Algonquin word for "fisher," which became the more Anglicized syllables "wood" and "chuck." Earlier, the similar forms "woodshock" and "woodshaw" occasionally were heard.

The standard dictionaries of Americanisms, terms coined or used principally in America, furnish additional hints on the history of the various names for the Groundhog. One of the earliest such dictionaries, John Russell Bartlett's *Dictionary of Americanisms* (1848), contains an early reference to the Groundhog under the listing for "woodchuck." This is his definition, borrowed from Webster: "In New England, the popular name of a rodent mammal, a species of the marmot tribe of animals, the *Arctomys monax*. It burrows and is dormant in winter." As a literary source, Bartlett quotes the novel *Margaret*, "Yea, verily, this is like a woodchuck in clover."

In *A Dictionary of Americanisms on Historical Principles* (1951), Mitford M. Mathews cites the entry for the Groundhog in Johan Frederick Bense, *A Dictionary of the Low-Dutch Element in the English Vocabulary* (1939), stating that "Bense may be correct in his surmise that this term was 'formed after the word *aard-vark* from Dutch *aard-varken*.'" Aardvark means "earth pig," although it appears to be used only in South Africa for an animal quite distinct from the Groundhog.

The earliest reference to the Groundhog that Mathews cites is dated 1656 and comes from a Dutchman named Van der Donck, who reported that "ground hogs, English skunks, drummers, and several other kinds of animals . . . are known and found in the country." Filson's *Kentucke* (1784) says: "Nor are the animals common to other parts wanting, such as foxes, . . . raccoons, ground-hogs, pole-cats, and opossums." Patrick Gass's Journal of 1807, reporting on his travels among the Indians, mentions seeing an Indian robe "made of ground hog skins." And finally, William H. Egle's *Notes and Queries* (1890) offers a Pennsylvania reference: "The groundhog is very numerous in Lancaster county, and in some of our rural districts is a positive pest, playing havoc with the young clover crop, and in the proper season it is a common thing for our 'crack shots' to bag a score of them in a single day." An amusing political reference to Groundhog Day, and one of the earliest recorded from the Midwest, was published in the *Chicago Tribune* on April 26, 1893: "It looks as though that political groundhog, the Hon. Bill Springer, had seen his own shadow about March 4, and had gone back into his hole to stay for four years."

A Groundhog foraging in the fields. ROUGHWOOD COLLECTION

The curious term *whistle pig*, the name for the Groundhog in some areas, is discussed in Mathews, giving evidence from West Virginia and the Great Smoky Mountain area of the South. The *Randolph Enterprise* (Elkins, West Virginia) on November 28, 1929, mentioned that "the whistle pig is taking his nap of six months." And Roderick Peattie, in *The Great Smokies and the Blue Ridge* (1943), furnishes this reference: "Whether the ground hog (called 'whistle-pig' by the mountain people of the Smokies) does or does not see his shadow on Candlemas Day isn't important"– a statement on which we obviously disagree.

The term *woodchuck* which is used all over New England and in New York State, and is occasionally heard in Pennsylvania, was documented in New England in the seventeenth century, as early as 1674. Mathews has a few references to the word. A "land of woodchucks" is a country area. And he informs us that "one woodchuck may eat as much as two pounds of greens in a day." Checking the packaged salad bins in my local supermarket I can only add, that's a lot of greens!

Science and the Groundhog Mythology

Occasionally, alternating with glowing newspaper reports of Groundhog Day festivities, scientific criticism of Groundhog legendry appears in the press. Such articles characteristically give a no-nonsense analysis of the Groundhog's actions and are usually based on the work of biologists who study Groundhogs or meteorologists who study the weather. They strike a sober note in our otherwise festive treatment of the Groundhog and his day, but they are important and should therefore be included.

A recent example is an article by Anthony R. Wood, "More Winter Hinges on Air Patterns, Not Groundhog's Shadow," which appeared in the February 2, 2001, *Philadelphia Inquirer.*

The evidence cited is from Wayne Higgins, a meteorologist at the U.S. Climate Prediction Center who keeps careful watch on the Arctic Oscillation, a pattern of air pressure and wind that is believed to be responsible for occurrences of frigid and mild weather in this country, including a series of mild winters in the 1990s.

According to Higgins, warmer winter weather in North America is caused by strong polar winds that trap cold air at the North Pole. When polar winds are weak, cold air near the Arctic Circle leaks southward, making North America colder. While this phenomenon results in what sort of winter weather Canada and the United States get, the Arctic Oscillation itself is unpredictable, changing from day to day and week to week. Hence it can't be used for forecasting winter weather, like the Groundhog, but can only explain it after it changes.

The Groundhog, the Farmer, and the Gardener

To farmers and gardeners, Groundhogs are not exactly popular neighbors, and they do not idealize or romanticize them. Richard Strickland, owner of Richland Farms in Bedford County, in an interview with Jon Fleck of the Altoona *Mirror* in 2003, called them "nasty little buggers." They are voracious herbivores that can devastate hay or crop fields, kitchen gardens, orchards, and nurseries. They are especially fond of Strickland's soybeans.

"In the summertime, it's not uncommon to find a circle around their hole with a radius of up to 100 feet they've nibbled out," Strickland says. Their burrows are a menace, too. "In the hay field, the holes are hard to see. Running into them damages the equipment." Even all-terrain vehicles can flip over if they hit a Groundhog hole, and horses and cattle have been known to break legs when stepping into them.

Stam Zervanos, assistant professor of biology at Penn State's Reading campus, was also interviewed by Fleck on the Groundhog problem. "I have yet to meet a farmer who likes them," he says. "Mainly, their diet consists of grasses and small herbs, but a garden is like setting up a buffet for them. It's not their normal diet, but it's easily accessible." Zervanos is currently studying forty-eight Groundhogs in a nearby 120-acre area to determine how they can be controlled. To curtail Groundhog damage, farmers sometimes have them shot or gassed, although these methods cannot be used in residential areas. Fencing the garden helps; Zervanos recommends that the fence be buried at least six inches deep. To relocate them, live traps can be used.

Not Weather but Love on Prognosticator's Mind?

An amusing Penn State release that circulated in January 2003 suggests that the Groundhog wakes up in early February each year to prepare for Valentine's Day.

According to Zervanos, who has spent several years studying the resident Groundhogs on a university farm near the Reading campus, the males and females stay apart during most of the year. "They're anti-social and, in fact, if they do come across each other they're sort of aggressive." He says that part of the reason they come out of their burrows at this time of year is so that the males can check out the available females.

Going into hibernation early in November, the male Groundhogs emerge from their burrows in early February to explore their territory and pay preliminary visits to the burrows of area females. These exploratory visits sometimes last two days, during which the male and female get acquainted, but they do not mate at this time. Mating takes place in early March, at the end of the actual hibernation period. The gestation period is thirty days, and the young are born in April. The Groundhog is territorial, largely keeping other males out of his territory, although more study is needed to determine whether the male mates with the same female visited in February.

Thus scientific investigators agree that the Groundhog, for whatever purpose, does emerge from his burrow in early February.

CHAPTER V

Groundhog Lodges

In the Pennsylvania Dutch Country, in Southeastern and parts of Central Pennsylvania, the Groundhog Day mystique has resulted in an innovative, all-dialect institution, the Groundhog Lodge. Through this creation, the Groundhog has become the principal symbol of the Pennsylvania Dutchman. The only competitor of the Groundhog may be the bearded Amishman, who has become a national figure growing out of Pennsylvania-centered twentieth-century tourism. Among thousands of dialect-speaking Dutchmen and their wives, the Groundhog is a potent, if tongue-in-cheek, symbol of the Dutchman himself.

The Pennsylvania Dutchman's relation to humor often focuses on the dialect. A long list of dialect humorists in the nineteenth and twentieth centuries operated under colorful, self-chosen pen names–Pit Schweffelbrenner (Pete Sulfurburner), Obediah Grouthomel (Cabbagecalf), Solly Hulsbuck (Solomon Sawhorse), Gottlieb Boonastiel (Beanpole), Ondreas Hussasock (Pantspocket), and numerous others just as witty. These pen name personalities are seen as symbols of the Pennsylvania Dutchman himself. The dialect literature produced in the last two centuries–books, pamphlets, broadsides, and countless "Letters to the Editor" of the upstate weekly newspapers–deal realistically with the faults and virtues of the Pennsylvania Dutchman. Hence, in a very real sense, this dialect literature can be considered a humorous, clever self-portrait of the Pennsylvania Dutch people themselves.

From this dialect-centered humor, it was only a short step to seeing the Groundhog–personified and humanized in the Groundhog Lodges–as an ethnic identity symbol of the Pennsylvania Dutch. As the Brother Groundhogs sing at their Lodges:

Liever Gott im Himmel drin,	Dear God up there in Heaven,
Loss uns Deitsche was mir sin;	Keep us Dutchmen as we are!
Und erhalt uns alle zeit	And keep alive forevermore
Unser Deitsche Freelichkeit!	The joyfulness we Dutchmen share.

Pumpernickle Bill

William S. Troxell (1893–1957), a dyed-in-the-wool Dutchman from Rising Sun in Lehigh County, deserves most of the credit for organizing the first *Grundsow Lodge* among the Pennsylvania Dutch. Like Clymer Freas of Punxsutawney and George Washington Hensel Jr. of Quarryville, he was a journalist, with a wide-ranging interest in his surroundings and the culture in which he grew up.

Troxell was raised in a dialect-speaking family, and when he became a country schoolteacher in Deibert's Valley, he was still living on the family farm. Every evening after supper, his father read to the family the dialect sketches in the Allentown *Morning Call* by "Obediah Grouthomel," a local named Solomon DeLong. DeLong encouraged Troxell to write dialect, and when he died, Troxell took over the column with the pen name of "Pumpernickle Bill."

With his popular column that appeared in the *Call* six times a week for more than thirty years, Troxell deserves the title of the most prolific writer of the dialect of all time. A tribute to Troxell by Lehigh Countian Alfred L. Shoemaker calls him the "Dean of Pennsylvania Dutch columnists." The column was witty and personal, based on Troxell's frequent travels through rural Lehigh and Northampton Counties, talking to people and gathering lore and reminiscences. His scholarly production was also considerable. With his close friend the Rev. Thomas R. Brendle, pastor of the historic Egypt Reformed Church, he traveled through Eastern and Central Pennsylvania gathering folksongs and folktales. He also edited a charming little book called *Aus Pennsylfawnia*, a collection of translations into Pennsylvania Dutch.

Troxell was first and foremost a man of the people. Interested in preserving his Dutch language and culture, he organized the Labor Day Schnitzing Parties and Applebutter Boilings at Dorney Park near Allentown, where dialect programs were presented. When the Folk Festival Movement began in Pennsylvania, he organized and directed,

The original Pennsylvania Dutch Groundhog Lodge first met in Northampton, Pennsylvania, on Groundhog Day 1934. Today there are nineteen of them. According to the history of *Grundsow Lodge Nummer Ains on da Lechaw* (Groundhog Lodge Number One on the Lehigh), the first planning session was held in Allentown at the home of "Pumpernickle Bill," newspaperman William S. Troxell. In attendance were the Reverend Thomas R. Brendle of the Egypt Reformed Church, renowned Pennsylvania Dutch folklorist and historian; Edgar Balliet of Northampton; and Harry Spannuth of Allentown. A committee of thirteen was appointed, and a little festival was held at the Keystone Trail Inn in Allentown on April 3, 1933.

William S. Troxell, "Pumpernickle Bill," with fellow Groundhogs of Lodge Number One. CARL D. SNYDER COLLECTION

in association with George Korson's statewide festivals, the regional Pennsylvania German Folk Festival held at Allentown, Pennsylvania, June 26–27, 1936. All of these gatherings were a primary root of the larger Pennsylvania Dutch Folk Festivals that began in 1949–1950.

In addition to all his other projects, Troxell also conducted a dialect radio program each week for some years, as well as serving as president of the Pennsylvania German Society from 1952 to 1957. With all his creative activities, including his formative influence on the Groundhog Lodge Movement, he can certainly be considered one of the leading figures in the Pennsylvania Dutch Renaissance of the 1930s.

First Fersammling *of Groundhog Lodge Number One on the Lehigh, February 2, 1934.* CARL D. SNYDER COLLECTION

The first great festival was held on Groundhog Day, February 2, 1934, in the Republican Club Rooms in Northampton. Nearly three hundred men attended, all of whom took the Groundhog Oath administered by Chairman Edgar Balliet and became charter members of *Grundsow Lodge Nummer Ains.* The lodge was fully organized with proper bylaws, and officers were voted in: Edgar Balliet, *Habtmon* (Chairman); Pumpernickle Bill, *Schreiver* (Secretary); Charles Oswald, *Geldhaver* (Treasurer); and Harvey Hankee, *Fuder Maishder* (Fodder Master). The *Rawd* (council) was made up of Thomas Brendle, Julius Lentz, Preston Barba, Mark Hoffman, Elmer Fehnel, Wilson Bilheimer, Samuel Brader, Milton Herber, and Clinton Knoll. The rest of the evening was spent in enjoying a program entirely in Pennsylvania Dutch, and all the members had an unusually good time. Dr. Edwin J. Fogel of Fogelsville gave the keynote speech, *"Hinner Grund fon da Penn.-Deitcha"* ("The Background of the Pennsylvania Dutch").

The Second Annual Assembly and Festival of *Grundsow Lodge Nummer Ains on da Lechaw* was held on February 4, 1935, the Monday after Groundhog Day, in the Masonic Temple at Allentown. The program was a full one, beginning with the singing of "America" in Pennsylvania Dutch and an opening prayer by Pastor William O. Wolford. This was followed by a reception of new members; music by Fenstermacher's *Deitschie Band*; the history of the lodge, given by the Chairman; the Key of Welcome tendered in Dutch by Allentown's dialect-fluent mayor, Fred Lewis; the reading of the bylaws; the singing of the Groundhog Song; and the Groundhog's Prophecy.

After the singing of *"Du, Du liegst mir im Herzen,"* the keynote address was given by the Honorable Frank M. Trexler, President Judge of Lehigh County, then *"O Adoline"* was sung. Dutch poems were read by Ralph Funk and John Birmelin, well-known dialect poets of the time, and after the singing of the "Lauterbach" song, a Dutch comedy was presented called *"'M Dr. Helfrich sei Office Schtunn"* (Dr. Helfrich's Office Hour), written by John Birmelin and performed by the Muhlenberg College Players, with Dr. Preston A. Barba as Dr. Helfrich. The evening closed with a rousing rendition of the *"Schnitzelbank"* song. Dinner was served, the high point being roast Lehigh Valley Groundhog (see the menu on page 92).

There are now nineteen Groundhog Lodges in the Pennsylvania Dutch area, as well as sixteen similar gatherings simply called *"Fersammlinge,"* meaning "meetings" or "gatherings." These are usually attended by several hundred people, and newspaper reports of their programs are published in the major local papers, sometimes even in the dialect. I had the honor of giving the keynote address at the *Barricks Caunty* (Berks County) *Fersammling* of 1983, the great tricentennial year celebrating the three hun-

 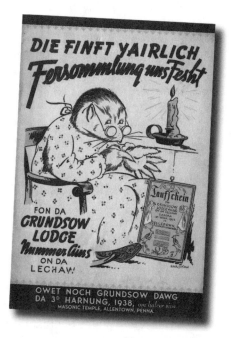

Early programs of Groundhog Lodge Number One on the Lehigh. ROUGH-WOOD COLLECTION

dredth anniversary of the planting of the first German-speaking settlement in the New World, Germantown. I called my effort *"En Gebottsdag-Gruss far die Pennsylfawnisch-Deitscha"* ("A Birthday Greeting for the Pennsylvania Dutch"). The Berks and Lehigh County papers published digests of the speech, and my Dutch must have been understood, since the reporters that were sent to cover the event even laughed at my jokes and reported them.

Whether called *Fersammlinge* or Groundhog Lodges, these Pennsylvania Dutch evenings are hilarious occasions, looked forward to all year by the participants. Dutch is spoken all evening, by everyone, and persons who slip into English are fined, good-humoredly. If some of the jokes told in the dialect are on the raunchy, risqué side, the laughter shows that they are appreciated, and indeed, the Pennsylvania Dutch enjoy sexual and scatological humor, as did their farmer forefathers and their peasant ancestry in Europe.

The wider meaning of the *Fersammling-Grundsow Lodge* movement—beyond the humor, the hearty consumption of Dutch soul food, and the singing of favorite dialect songs—was captured in the *American-German Review* for June–August 1947 in these important words:

> The twentieth century revival of interest in the history and culture of the Pennsylvania German has assumed the proportions of a folk movement of considerable magnitude. Especially is this true when one observes the many gatherings at which the dialect is spoken to the complete exclusion of the English language. These gatherings take on varied forms. In Allentown, Skippack and Philadelphia Candlemas Day, or Groundhog Day, is observed on February 2 each year. In a spirit of fun the Pennsylvania Germans of today capitalize upon the superstitions of their forebears and in serio-comic style do homage to the lowly beast, the groundhog, paying tribute to his weather wisdom.

A Tribute to the Fersammling Movement

A somewhat defensive tribute to the dialect *Fersammling* movement had appeared earlier in the Lebanon *Semi-Weekly News* for March 28, 1940. The article presents a good summary of the early development of the dialect movement and points out that the first such gathering to be organized was the Snyder County *Fersammling* at Selinsgrove (1932). It doesn't mention the *Grundsow Lodges*, although it does include a reference to the now famous "Deitsch Jubilee" Picnics in Jefferson County–Groundhog territory par excellence. The article was thought important enough as an expression of opinion to be reprinted in the October 1940 *American-German Review* and in Homer T. Rosenberger's *The Pennsylvania Germans, 1891–1965.*

The defensive note is struck in the final two paragraphs of the article. This was written only a year before the outbreak of World War II, when Pennsylvania Dutchmen were trying to prove how American they really were. Hitler's Germany was at the time causing deep concern among many groups in the United States. While there was little evidence then of anti-German feeling against the Pennsylvania Germans, who had been on American soil since 1683, the author of this thoughtful article deemed it wise to underline the basic Americanism of the Pennsylvania Dutch. That this Americanism was strongly expressed in the all-dialect *Grundsow Lodge* and *Fersammling* movement is clear.

> While all of these groups differ in many respects they are alike in that they represent an organized effort to reclaim our heritage as a distinct American group. Here we have a group of people whose ancestors were among the earliest settlers of America. For more than two hundred years they have taken a vital part in the building of America, just as they strove to make her independent. They have fought her battles and have obeyed her laws and have loved her better than life itself. Politically they have cast off every vestige of the lands of their origins. If the Pennsylvania Germans are not Americans THEN THERE ARE NO AMERICANS.
>
> Let no man impute false motives to this movement. He who even suggests that any but the most patriotic motives pervade all of these gatherings utters a base calumny born of sinister purpose or of pitiable ignorance. What could be more impressive than a thousand men and women who with their ancestors have an aggregate of a quarter of a million years on American soil standing while they sing AMERICA in their own Pennsylvania German dialect?

Female Groundhog Lodges

In recent years, the Groundhog Lodge Movement has come under criticism from the Pennsylvania Dutch *Weibsleit* (women), who insist that since there must be female *Grundsei* (the plural term for groundhogs), and the lodge membership is limited to men only, there should also be Groundhog

Lodges for women. Two of these have been organized and are now in full operation: *Die Weibsleit Grundsow Lodge fon da Baryomadahl* (the Upper Perkiomen Ladies *Grundsow Lodge*) at East Greenville in Montgomery County, led by Lucy J. Kern, and the *Drei County Weibsleit Fersommling* (Tri-County Women's Assembly) at Fogelsville in Lehigh County, led by Lillie George.

A program of the Upper Perkiomen Ladies Lodge for Tuesday, April 20, 1993, held in the East Greenville Fire Hall, predictably praises the Pennsylvania Dutch and their cookery. Typical lodge activities were featured: singing "America" and pledging allegiance to the flag, both in Dutch; reciting the Lord's Prayer, showing the connection between ethnic identity and religion; and serving a delicious meal for which all the cooks were applauded. The high point of the evening was a Dutch play, evidently by Carl Arner, with the humorous title *"Der Chorch Washington, Gummschtiwwel Un So Sache in Die Chapel Schuul"* ("George Washington, Gum Boots and Such Things in the Chapel School"). It was undoubtedly an enjoyable evening.

Groundhog Lodge Humor

In the popular column *"Scholla,"* which appeared three times a week in the Reading *Times*, Arthur Dundore Graeff (1899–1969), a Berks County Dutchman, educator, historian, and dialect poet, reported and commented on many aspects of Pennsylvania Dutch folk culture. According to Graeff, the word *Scholla* means "echoes," as in "echoes from the past." The column ran from 1938 to 1969, appearing in more than four thousand issues. In it, Graeff frequently reported the humorous goings-on at the various Groundhog Lodges he attended.

Characteristically, the addresses delivered at the Groundhog Lodges are slanted toward humor and satire. A column entitled "Weather Wisdom," published in the February 27, 1952, *Times*, reports on the striking presentation made by Dr. Harry Hess Reichard of Muhlenberg College at the annual Groundhog Banquet held in 1952 at Temple University in Philadelphia.

Speaking in his fluent Lehigh County Dutch, Reichard expounded the theory that humankind has survived through the millennia, and indeed "triumphed, over other animals because he was alert enough to study weather conditions and protect himself accordingly." Human beings have gained this power "by watching the other animals and combining the many bits of weather wisdom which they revealed." He depicted Adam in para-

The Pennsylvania Dutch Groundhog Lodges

How many Pennsylvania Dutch Groundhog Lodges are there? With the Delaware Lodge disbanded and the No. 3 at Temple University in Philadelphia inactive, the number of lodges is currently nineteen. They are as follows:

No. 1 on the Lehigh, Allentown

No. 2 on the Skippack, Souderton

No. 4 on the Tohickon, Quakertown

No. 5 on the Swatara, Pine Grove

No. 6 at Brodheadsville, Monroe County

No. 7 at East Greenville, Montgomery County

No. 8 on the Lizard Creek, Schuylkill County

No. 9 in Dublin, Bucks County

No. 10 at Stroudsburg, Monroe County

No. 11 at Fire Line, Carbon County

No. 12 on the Tulpehocken Path, Berks County

No. 13 on Indian Creek, Emmaus

No. 14 on Saucon Creek, Coopersburg

No. 15 at Kutztown, Berks County

No. 16 on the Jordan, Allentown

No. 17 at Myerstown, Lebanon County

No. 18 on Big Trout Creek, Emerald

Upper Perkiomen (Ladies Grundsow Lodge)

Fogelsville (Tri-County Women's Assembly)

All of these lodges hold annual meetings, with all the Groundhog hoopla and fun-making, and publish annual programs mostly in Pennsylvania Dutch, including songs and illustrated with amusing cartoons. I have translated into English all of the official titles of the lodges, which are in Pennsylvania Dutch.

dise "watching the swallows return to the barn before he planted his potatoes." Noah watched the bees to learn that a storm was coming, and after the flood, "watched the dove for a sign that the waters were receding." There was also that "Greek high school teacher named Aristotle" who "worked out an almanac by which men could know the future of the

weather according to a series of signs and symbols." He even cited Jesus as paying attention to signs in the sky, and quoted Shakespeare. All this led up to the usual peroration on the Groundhog as weather prophet and the sanctity, for Pennsylvania Dutchmen, of Groundhog Day.

The *"Scholla"* offering for March 19, 1958, reports that one of the best jokes perpetrated at a Groundhog Lodge involved a live Groundhog being placed on the speaker's table and "offered a choice between eating dry shoo-fly or wet shoo-fly, his choice of the two symbolizing the weather prospect." Alas, the visitor "ate both pies with relish and then turned over and fell asleep while the solons pondered the meaning of his behavior." Their conclusion? Groundhogs like shoo-fly pie!

The humor of the Groundhog Lodges was kept up-to-date by reflecting things that were going on in the outside world. In 1968, when hippies and flower children were attracting national attention, one of the Pennsylvania Dutch Groundhog Lodges featured at its annual banquet an interview with a Hippie Groundhog waving a flower in its paw, showing off its extralong hair, and reciting poetry in broken Dutch. Among its pronouncements was *"Halt's kiehl, Mann!"* which was translated, "Keep it cool, man." Did he mean six more weeks of winter? the officers asked. But then the guest uttered, *"Alles iss wie's sei sett"* ("All will be groovy"), which could imply an early spring. At any rate, the humor was from the modern world but expressed in the traditional language of the Pennsylvania Dutch.

The Typical Groundhog Lodge Program

In each of the sessions of all nineteen Groundhog Lodges, the Groundhog mystique is featured year after year. It's a fun thing, with three or four hundred or more male *Grundsei*—and a few female ones—to take on the role of the weather-predicting Groundhog. Whether they wear top hats and formal garb or don Groundhog Caps for the occasion, they act out the role of the Groundhog weather prophet.

The program format that has been developed over the almost seven decades since the first Dutch Groundhog Lodge, *Grundsow Lodge Num-*

Lodge members raise their paws to take the Sacred Groundhog Oath, 2003.
CARL D. SNYDER COLLECTION

mer Ains on da Lechaw, was founded in Allentown, is now standard. Beginning the evening with singing "America" in the fluent Dutch translation by John Birmelin, followed by a Dutch prayer by a local or imported clergyman, the assembled brethren sing Groundhog and other dialect songs and listen to *Grundsow Dawg Barichda* (Groundhog Day Reports). Then the *Habtman* (lodge chairman) gives the *Amtlich Wedder-Brophetzeiing* (Official Weather Prophecy). In some lodges, the new members raise their "paws" and take a Groundhog Oath, and in some cases the officers issue a *Grundsau Daag Proclamation*. The sidebar gives an example of one such proclamation, issued for the 1952 session of Groundhog Lodge Number One on the Lehigh by *Habtman* Irwin J. Frantz and *Schreiwer* (Secretary) Pumpernickle Bill, Allentown newspaperman William S. Troxell.

Grundsow Dawg Proclamation

To the members of Grundsow Lodge Nummer Ains on da Lechaw, Greetings:

Be it hereby known that I, Irwin J. Frantz, habtman of this exalted lodge, do hereby enjoin every member to observe this day in the following manner:

1. Rise before daybreak, partake of no nourishing food and talk to nobody for fear of getting misleading information. Forget any conversations you may overhear so your mind will not be polluted by false predictions.

2. Now proceed to the Groundhog hole, equipped with paper and pencil. Take accurate observation of the atmospheric ceiling, direction and velocity of wind and time of day. Be sure hole is in middle of field, at least 200 yards from any fenceline, tree or building so that shadow is not disturbed. Record actions of Mr. Groundhog so that proper predictions can be made.

3. During rest of the day, stay close to nature and refuse to listen to untrustworthy and unjust reports. When the sun has set next Monday, take a bath, dress in clean clothes and solemnly follow the trail traveled by the Rawd [Council] to the Frolics Ballroom to hear the report of observations and the prediction of type of weather that may be expected the next six weeks.

Given under my hand and the great seal of the Lodge this first day of February of the good year of 1952, being the 18th year of the founding of Our Esteemed Lodge and the 16th of the annual meeting.

Pumpernickle Bill Schreiwer
Irwin J. Frantz Habtman

The Lodge Movement and the Dutch Dialect

Not only has the Groundhog become the principal symbol of the Pennsylvania Dutchman through the widespread Groundhog Lodge Movement, but the lodges also help promote and foster the Pennsylvania Dutch language. All the evening's proceedings are in Dutch, and those unwary Brother Groundhogs who are caught talking English are fined anywhere from 10 to 36 cents, according to the rules of various lodges. The money collected is given to local charities. In addition, the lodges provide occasions for the playing and singing of Pennsylvania Dutch instrumental music and songs, both traditional Dutch folksongs and Dutch translations of contemporary pop-culture songs.

Several popular local bands furnish music for the Groundhog Lodges' evening parties, including the *Leroy Heffentrager Buwe* (Heffentrager's Boys), sometimes called *Heffie un sei Buwe* (Heffie and His Boys); *'M Fenstermacher sei Deitschie Band* (Fenstermacher's Dutch Band); and the versatile Wolfe Family of Gratz, Dauphin County, who play instrumental music and sing highly amusing songs of their own composition. Dutch singing groups, mostly quartets, also enliven the festive evenings. These include *Die Bernviller Singer* (The Bernville Singers), from Western Berks County; *Die Freindlicha Fiera* (The Friendly Four), of Pine Grove, Schuylkill County; and *Die Schwillie Willies*, from Montgomery County.

Among the dialect folksongs that appear in text in many Groundhog Lodge programs are some old standards, such as *"Schpinn, Schpinn, Meine Liewi Dochter"* ("Spin, Spin, My Dear Daughter"); *"Hei Lie Hei Lo,"* with a yodel chorus threaded into a multitude of witty, impromptu verses (some rather risqué); the universally beloved *"Lauterbach"* song, also with a yodel chorus; and *"All die Deitsche Brieder"* ("All the Dutch Brethren"), a nineteenth-century drinking song. There are also local songs, such as *"Der Bella Baum"* ("The Tulip Tree") and *"Wu Iss Dann die Mary?"* ("Just Where Is Mary?"), who turns out to be *"drunne in Macungie"* ("down in Macungie"), a town in Lehigh County.

Many pop-culture songs are translated into Pennsylvania Dutch, or Dutch words are fitted to pop tunes. Examples are *"Good-bye, Susanna, Good-bye,"* to the tune of "Good-bye, My Lover, Goodbye"; *"Wart Bis Die Sunn Scheint, Nellie"* ("Wait 'Til the Sun Shines, Nelly"); *"O Adeline, O Adeline"*; *"Lang Lang Zurick,"* beginning, *"Sing mir en Schtick vun lang lang zurick"* ("Sing me a piece from long, long ago"); *"Die Bolly Melinda,"* to the tune of "Sweet Rosie O'Grady"; *"Die Alt Groe Maar"* ("The Old Gray Mare") which "iss net was sie alfart wor" ("is not what she used to be"); *"Der Meh Mir Kumma Tzamma"* ("The More We Get Together"); and *"Daheem Uff die Alt Bauerei"* ("Home on the Old Farm"), to the tune of "Home on the Range."

Occasionally the translations sung at the Groundhog Lodges are hymns or gospel songs. Among these are Pastor Ralph Starr's translation of "I Need Thee Every Hour" *("Ich Brauch Dich Alle Schtunn")* and Arthur D. Graeff's translation of "How Great Thou Art" *("Wie Gross Du Bischt")*.

And usually one or two songs are lustily sung in praise of being Dutch, or talking the beloved mother tongue *(Mudder-Schprooch)*. One of these is the very popular *"Deitsch Schwetza un Singa,"* sung to the tune of "Springtime in the Rockies." It begins with the thought: *"Oh, ich gleich des Deitsch zu schwetza, Ya, es iss mei Mudder Schprooch"* ("Oh, I like to talk Dutch, yes, it is my mother tongue").

In the hilarious camaraderie of the *Grundsow Lodges*, the use of English was cordially forbidden so that the assembled Groundhogs could *schwetz* (talk) their *Deitsch* all evening. For some, as at the lodge convening at Temple University in Philadelphia, this meant polishing up the childhood speech that they had left behind in the farming valleys of the Dutch Country when they went away to college and got work in the city. By using the Pennsylvania Dutch language all evening, singing Dutch songs together, and listening to all the humorous speeches and jokes, the lodges provide a way of reinforcing their Pennsylvania Dutch identity, their consciousness of who they are.

Most of the lodges humorously fine the brethren who let English words slip out during the proceedings. This warning appears in the program of the Monroe County Groundhog Lodge for 1988: *"Breeder Grundsi, Nemma Des in Ocht: English Schwetze kosh'd Gelt–10 Cents 'S Wert, All Bens Shtrofe Gelt gait Tzum 'Charity'"* ("Brother Groundhogs, watch out! Talking English costs money–10 cents a word. All the money from these penny fines goes to charity").

Like other Americans, Pennsylvania Dutchmen seek and enjoy membership in secret or open organizations with fraternal handshakes, oaths, and identification with the organizational symbol. In the nineteenth and twentieth centuries, Pennsylvania Dutchmen delighted in joining fraternal organizations, such as the Masons, Odd Fellows, Elks, and Moose, as well as the Groundhog Lodges.

Brother Groundhogs of Lodge Number One on February 2, 1994. CARL D. SNYDER COLLECTION

Apart from its indirect connection to the American fraternal orders of the nineteenth century, the Lodge Movement derives directly from the Quarryville Slumbering Groundhog Lodge of 1908. Making the organization a lodge, with oaths and other accoutrements of the typical American fraternal organizations, was a clever takeoff on the format of the earlier Punxsutawney Groundhog Club of 1886. The focusing of the Pennsylvania Dutch Groundhog Lodges on the Dutch dialect and group identity was a master stroke that has enabled the movement to continue down through the decades into the present century. As long as there are speakers of Dutch who want to assemble with others and enjoy the annual festivities, the movement will undoubtedly continue.

On the other hand, while the whole Groundhog Day mystique was a Pennsylvania Dutch contribution to the state and nation, neither the Punxsutawney nor the Quarryville celebrations emphasize Pennsylvania Dutchness. Some of the Punxsutawney club members and most of the Quarryville lodge participants bear Pennsylvania Dutch names, but alas, in present-day Jefferson County and Southern Lancaster County near the Maryland border, the Dutch language is no longer a feature of the cultural landscape. Still, despite this shift in emphasis, we can continue to claim Punxsutawney newspaperman Freas, who shaped it all up in the late nineteenth century, and his Quarryville counterpart Hensel, as part of the Pennsylvania Dutch cultural world.

Professor Alvin F. Kemp, a dyed-in-the-wool Berks County Dutchman who served as superintendent of schools for Berks County in the 1940s, compiled an analysis of the Dutch dialect institutions in his perceptive article "The Pennsylvania German Versammlinge" (1944). He dealt with twenty-two organizations that held dialect meetings over twelve counties of Pennsylvania, dividing them into five related types: Versammlinge Proper, Grundsow Lodges, Church Versammlinge (Dialect Church Services), Folk Festivals, and Summer Versammlinge and Picnics.

His conclusions about the significance of the Lodge Movement for the Pennsylvania Dutch were that the lodges provided wholesome entertainment, a substantial Pennsylvania Dutch meal, familiarity with the history and traditions of the Pennsylvania Dutch, appreciation of their folklore, renewed pride "in the soul" of the Pennsylvania Dutch, "curbing of unjust and undeserved criticism of writers and speakers," and revitalization of the dialect.

The belief that Groundhog Lodges strengthened the Pennsylvania Dutch sense of cultural identity is echoed in the excellent recent history of the movement by anthropologist William W. Donner of Kutztown University. Professor Donner sees the lodge sessions, apart from "being a lot of fun for the participants," as "rare examples of an ongoing folk tradition in American culture."

> The main speeches are humorous, sometimes racy, but they also usually include a moral message for the listeners (many of the Grundsow speakers are from the clergy), often with references to the importance and strengths of traditional Pennsylvania German cultural practices. The skits are written and performed by members and often include some social commentary presented through humor. It is rare in our modern culture to find examples of speech performances, plays and visual displays that are not developed or dominated by professional media for commercial interests. But the Grundsow meetings are performed by local people, to preserve a regional dialect and culture, and maintained year to year by the participants themselves.

The analysis continues with the important statement that the "style of performed humor" in the Groundhog Lodges "derives from earlier periods in American life, before the saturation of mass media, when people entertained one another through telling jokes, stories and live performances."

> The main character, King Groundhog, remains true to his folk roots, whereas his much better known cousin, Punxsutawney Phil, has become completely commercialized into a national media event, and even appeared in a Hollywood movie. The lodge meetings are cultural and linguistic preservation movements, continuing not only a language but also a style of oral presentation.

Totemism and New Folklore

The phenomenon of the Pennsylvania Dutch Groundhog Lodge Movement can be explained by relating it to two very different cultural phenomena: totemism in primitive religion; and popular culture, the mass-media-controlled aspects of American culture today. As an identity symbol of the Pennsylvania Dutch people for the twentieth and twenty-first centuries, the

Loyal lodge members with token Groundhog. (Is he real or stuffed?) CARL D. SNYDER COLLECTION

anthropological concept of totemism can be applied. Totemic animals are those adopted and identified with by primitive peoples as symbols of their tribal identity. An example from Colonial Pennsylvania is the Turtle Tribe of the Delaware Indians.

The Groundhog has in a sense been adopted by the Pennsylvania Dutchman as his totemic or symbolic animal, without the magical trappings of primitive totemism. In the nineteenth- and twentieth-century burgeoning of fraternal orders for men in America, the Elks, Moose, and Groundhog Lodges of the Pennsylvania Dutch were structured in a semitotemic format. When a member of a Groundhog Lodge puts on a Groundhog Cap and takes the Groundhog Oath to be faithful to the principles of Groundhogism, is this not at least tongue-in-cheek totemism?

In primitive totemism, often either there was a taboo against eating the totemic animal, or the animal was ritually slain and eaten in a sacramental meal. Echoes of the latter approach can be found in the Groundhog

Program with Ground-hog and Pennsylvania Dutch flag, popular identity symbols for the lodges. CARL D. SNYDER COLLECTION

feasts held in the early days of the Punxsutawney Groundhog Club and in the first banquets staged by Allentown's Groundhog Lodge Number One on the Lehigh, where Groundhog was actually on the menu.

Totemism, whether primitive or tongue-in-cheek, relates man to the natural world in a basic way, based on a recognition of human relationships to the natural world. And most important of all, through the development of this mock-fraternal organization known as the Groundhog Lodge, the Groundhog has become the leading symbol of the Pennsylvania Dutch people.

It is true that the Groundhog Lodge Movement has helped preserve a vital American folk-cultural heritage. But this heritage has been drastically reshaped or retreaded by the powerful, media-driven popular culture of the twentieth and twenty-first centuries. In an essay published in 1971, "Pennsylvania German Folklore Research: A Historical Analysis," I describe the Grundsow Lodge and Fersammling movement as "New Folklore" institutions. By this I mean that while the lodges and assemblies derive some of their content from traditional folk culture, their format has been radically reshaped by the popular culture that surrounds us everywhere and invades our homes daily via radio, television, and computer screen, whether we speak Pennsylvania Dutch or not.

As "New Folklore" institutions, the lodges have over the years created new forms of Pennsylvania Dutch folklore. These have taken their place alongside the traditional lore and in some cases have superimposed themselves upon it. This is the case with the high pop-culture component found in the Groundhog Lodge and Fersammling song repertoire, striking every popular American note from *"Fergess net Pearl Harbor"* in 1941 to the all-time-favorite *"Dahame uff die alt Bauerei,"* Gilbert Snyder's somewhat ungrammatical translation of "Home on the Range." The "New Folklore" aspects of the lodge format are also seen in the humorous menus, with their new coinages of food terms, and in the humorous names for the officers of the lodges.

All of this can be seen as a potent illustration of radical Americanization, the thoroughgoing acculturation of the Pennsylvania Dutch to the popular culture surrounding them. I became aware of this general influence through my study of Pennsylvania Dutch cookbook literature. Most of the cookbooks compiled or issued by nonprofessionals include over-generous quantities of pop-culture foods. While these books show a token interest in traditional Dutch dishes, such as sauerkraut, scrapple, and

The Groundhog as totem. Members of Lodge Number One carry the Ground-hog to the stage at a recent session. CARL D. SNYDER COLLECTION

Schnitz un Gnepp, most of the pages are filled with what I call *Ladies Home Journal* and *Country Gentleman* recipes of the 1920s, including that American classic of classics, tuna and noodle casserole.

Viewing present-day Pennsylvania Dutch culture as combining traditional folk-cultural elements with pop-cultural phenomena, it can be seen as functioning in many layers. In this cultural stratigraphy, traditional elements of European lore, legend, and belief join hands with, or are subtly reshaped or retreaded into, new pop-culture formats. The traditional elements come from the very roots of the culture; the pop-culture elements come in from outside. Even the basic Pennsylvania Dutch language, the matrix of the traditional culture, is being reshaped by these external, general American influences.

CHAPTER VI

Groundhog
on the Table

In pioneer days, even in the woods of Jefferson County during the early nineteenth century, Groundhog was widely consumed in the log cabins along with other wild game. In those days, there were no supermarkets with tempting displays of fresh and frozen meats, hence Groundhog often appeared on the pioneer's table. It was, after all, quite edible flesh, from a clean-living, vegetarian creature that lived in neat burrows in the ground.

In his magisterial *Viviparous Quadrupeds of North America* (1846), John James Audubon writes that "the body of the wood-chuck is extremely flabby after being killed, its flesh is, however, tolerably good, although a little strong, and is frequently purchased by the humbler classes of people, who cook it like a roasting pig." Occasionally, however, especially in autumn, when the animal is getting ready for its winter hibernation, it is "exceedingly fat."

In an undated article from before 1920, included in Bill Anderson's *Groundhog Day, 1886–1992*, the Punxsutawney *Spirit* promoted the eating of Groundhog:

> As for groundhog itself—well, to fully appreciate its flavor—you first must taste it. Some say it resembles bear-steak, but it's better than bruin. There's a hint of red clover about it and a delicate reminder of aromatic roots. There is just enough of the game tinge to let you know you are eating outside the dooryard of domestication. . . . Before being cooked, the little prophet des-

tined for the picnic table is relieved of a small sac under one foreleg–this to avoid a strong taste that would doom his Seership as a table delicacy–and allowed to marinate overnight so that it is decidedly more palatable.

"Groundhog Dan's" Groundhog Stew

From Jefferson County, where Punxsutawney is now the recognized Groundhog Capital of the United States, comes a nostalgic reference to the famous Groundhog Stew served in the Snyder family of Dora, Pennsylvania, in the nineteenth and early twentieth centuries. Daniel S. Snyder (1837–1914), known as "Groundhog Dan," was evidently the principal maker. Dan was born in the Mahantongo Valley of Schuylkill County in Eastern Pennsylvania, son of Benjamin and Catharina (Hepler) Schneider, and came with his parents to Jefferson County in 1850 along with dozens of other Mahantongo families.

This Mahantongo settlement in southern Jefferson County, and the adjoining corners of Clarion, Indiana, and Armstrong Counties, made the area strongly Pennsylvania Dutch far into the last century, when the first of a series of Dutch Jubilee Picnics was held in 1935. The Groundhog Stew continued into the twentieth century, its taste remembered with lip-smacking affection. And "Groundhog Dan" had a son who was known as "Groundhog Jim."

Groundhogs enjoying a feast. ROUGHWOOD COLLECTION

Whistle Pigs on the Table

In poor farming areas of Pennsylvania, the Groundhog became a poverty food, a substitute for the meats that poor folk could neither raise nor afford to buy for their families. This is brought out in James York Glimm's charming 1983 book, *Flat-Landers and Ridge-Runners: Folktales from the Mountains of Northern Pennsylvania*. From Walter Thomas of Canton, Pennsylvania, he recorded the following:

> Back when I was small, my dad was a coal miner, and practically all through the summer months we lived on whistle pigs. That's what we called woodchucks. We also ate milkweed and polkgreens. You see, all the winter food was gone and the crops hadn't come in yet, so it was a hungry time. Many and many a Sunday we wouldn't have had meat if it weren't for the whistle pigs. We fixed the milkweed greens just like lettuce. You could either have it cold or hot with vinegar. What my mother used to do was put some vinegar and flour in. Kinda made a gravy.

Groundhog Memories from Centre County

Centre County, Pennsylvania, in the exact center of the state, is Groundhog country par excellence. My grandfather, Wharton Morris Cronister (1861–1945), former county sheriff and farmer at Martha Furnace in the Bald Eagle Valley, relished meals of roast Groundhog. I asked some of my cousins and longtime friends there what they remember about the Groundhog on the table.

One of my first cousins, Don Myers, a businessman of Philipsburg, in the high Allegheny Mountains of Centre County, was raised on a primitive farm in a narrow hollow back from the main floor of the Bald Eagle Valley, at Martha Furnace. Recently I asked Don if my Aunt Myra, his mother, ever cooked Groundhog. "Yes," he said, "we sure cooked Groundhog when I was a boy on the farm. We got them in the spring. We waited until the clover was in bloom, then they were OK to eat." He told me that Aunt Myra fried them. I asked him what they tasted like. "Well, they taste like Groundhog–kind of greasy like. They have a taste of their own–kind of a strong, greasy taste, but we enjoyed it. We ate a lot of them." Hunting them was quite an art. "We saw their holes all over the hills. Every once in a while, we'd shoot a young one. We'd watch for them. Sometimes after we shot at them, they'd crawl back into their holes and we'd have to dig them out, half dead if they were shot." Though I recall many delicious meals around Aunt Myra's pleasant table, it seems I was never there when Groundhog was the pièce de résistance.

One of the best cooks I remember from Centre County was Margaret Brugger Waite, a Bellefonte High School classmate and lifelong friend of my mother's. Margaret came from Unionville, and when I knew her, she lived on farms at Centre Line and Zion. Her husband, J. Earl Waite, was a farmer from Halfmoon Valley. I recently asked Margaret's daughter, Jane Waite Stover of Greensburg, if her mother ever cooked Groundhog. "Yes," Jane answered, "she cooked them for guests who liked them, like Orby Clark and Percy Harshberger. But she hated them herself, because they were greasy and stringy." When I asked how she cooked them, Jane told me she roasted them. Her father shot them, "but he would only shoot the young ones, in the spring."

Not all of my contacts confessed to having eaten Groundhog. When I asked L. Wilbur Zimmerman, age ninety-five, of Haverford, if he had ever eaten Groundhog, he replied, "No, but I knew people who did. I lived at Broomall in Delaware County for four years, 1916 to 1920, when it was still farmland—now it's about all suburbanized. Some of our farmer neighbors did eat Groundhog, but I was never personally tempted to partake of it."

The Groundhog in Nineteenth-Century Metropolitan Markets

Occasionally references to Groundhog and its culinary uses turn up in unexpected places. In Thomas F. DeVoe's *The Market Assistant* (1866), a best-seller in its day that purportedly describes "every article of human food sold in the public markets of the cities of New York, Boston, Philadelphia, and Brooklyn," with "many curious incidents and anecdotes," there is a chapter devoted to "Wild Animals, Called Game." After describing the culinary uses of deer, buffalo, antelope, sheep, goat, bear, rabbit, guinea pig, squirrel, raccoon, wildcat, and opossum, there is the following discussion of Woodchuck, or Groundhog:

> This small, stout, brown-colored animal is only occasionally seen in our markets, although often killed within twenty miles of the city of New York. In the fall months they are very fat, when the flesh of the young is quite palatable, somewhat like a pig, and is considered wholesome. The old ones are tolerably good, but much better after having been frozen some time. They usually weigh from eight to twelve pounds. A fine fat

young one, weighing six and a quarter pounds, dressed like a roasting-pig (hair scalded off), and much resembling that animal, was shown at Jefferson Market, August 17, 1860; it was shot at Throg's Neck, Westchester County, New York. In the *Deerfield News,* June 4, 1820 (Hampshire County, Mass.), is noticed–"Our famous woodchuck-hunt terminated, on Wednesday, in favor of the party under Mr. E. Nims, who destroyed one thousand one hundred and fifty-four. Those under Mr. J. C. Hoyt destroyed eight hundred and seventy-three–making a total of two thousand and twenty-seven!

The chapter continues with disquisitions on porcupine, skunk–"the flesh of this most detestable animal is, I am told, when properly prepared, as good as raccoon"–beaver, otter, badger, and finally, muskrat.

In a Chicago cookbook copyrighted 1884 and reissued in 1903, entitled *Mrs. Owens' Cook Book and Useful Household Hints,* there is an enthusiastic recipe for cooking Groundhog sent in by Mrs. E. E. Bower of Erie, Pennsylvania. Included in the chapter on "Game," it reads as follows:

In Pennsylvania, woodchucks are called ground-hogs and esteemed a great delicacy, and really a fine fat one well roasted is not to be despised. To cook either ground-hogs or 'coons [raccoons], parboil for 30 minutes, to take off the wild smell; then rub well with salt and pepper, and roast in a quick oven at first, allowing the fire to cool gradually; 30 minutes to every pound is a safe rule. Young animals need no parboiling. Where fire-places are used, people cook them on a spit over a dripping pan.

The compiler says in her preface, "The recipes in this book are National, having been gleaned from the extreme East, West, North and South, as well as from intermediate points." The recipes are actually very good, and it is delightful that she thought a Groundhog recipe worthy of inclusion.

Twentieth-Century Recipes

For what is evidently the most widespread recipe in print, Punxsutawney again takes the honors. In 1958, when the Groundhog Day festivity was firmly established and was spreading elsewhere, the Adrian Hospital Auxiliary of Punxsutawney compiled an attractive and witty cookbook, *Cooking with the Groundhog,* edited by Elaine Kahn Light and Ruth B. Hamill. This recipe, which has appeared widely in newspaper columns and other media across the state, follows:

Clean and dress an 8–10 pound groundhog. Be sure to remove the 7 to 9 white muscle-like sacs that are under the front legs and the small of the back. Cut in serving pieces and soak overnight in salted water. Boil the cleaned groundhog ½ hour in water seasoned with 1 tablespoon wine vinegar and 1 tablespoon soda. Drain well. Dredge meat in mixture of salt, pepper and paprika. Fry out some bacon and salt pork and sear meat in the rendered fat until it is well browned on all sides. Place meat in roaster with the drippings. Add 2 cloves garlic, 1 chopped onion, 3 table-spoons each chopped parsley, celery and carrots, 6 peppercorns, crushed, 2 cloves, 1 teaspoon thyme and salt to taste. Cover meat with 2 cups red wine and 2 cups beef stock (bouillon). Roast, covered, 1 hour at 350°F., then reduce heat to 250°F. until meat is tender, adding more beef stock as needed to prevent meat from becoming dry. About ½ hour before meat is done, sprinkle with 1 tablespoon of flour. Garnish with chopped parsley before serving.

In the February 2002 issue of the attractive monthly magazine *Hometown Punxsutawney*, an article by editor Terry A. Fye entitled "Ground-hog, Punx'y Style" appeared in his column, "In the Hometown Kitchen." The column opens with a description of another kind of roast—the Celebrity Roast involving "a group of witty friends gathering together to salute a comrade with a variety of sometimes embarrassing and ribald stories of the

Governor Edwin S. Stuart joins Groundhog Club president A. J. Truitt in a Groundhog feast, while Supreme Court Justice John P. Elkin comments on the dish, in this 1909 cartoon from the Philadelphia North American. PUNX-SUTAWNEY AREA HISTORICAL AND GENEALOGICAL SOCIETY

An argument over the best way to cook Groundhog from a cartoon in the Philadelphia North American.
PUNXSUTAWNEY AREA HISTORICAL AND GENEALOGICAL SOCIETY

honoree's climb to fame." Punxsutawney Phil "may well prefer that kind of gathering to the type of festivities that once greeted his ancestors," says Fye. Earlier, "the groundhog wasn't the center of attention; he was the center of the meal."

The recipe from *Cooking with the Groundhog* follows, and then, in case "a parboiled, fried groundhog isn't your idea of fine dining," Fye suggests whipping up a batch of the Punxsutawney specialty "Woodchucks," chewy, succulent cookies often baked in Groundhog-shaped molds that are sold in the town. This recipe is attributed to Margaret Wardrop Barilar.

> 2 cups walnut meats
> 1 cup dates
> 1 cup brown sugar, packed
> 2 eggs, slightly beaten
> 2¹/₂ cups shredded moist coconut
>
> Coarsely grind nuts and dates. Mix with sugar, eggs, and 1¹/₂ cups of coconut. Shape into ³/₄-by-2-inch oblong rolls. Roll in remaining cup of coconut. Bake on ungreased cookie sheet twelve to fifteen minutes at 375° F.
>
> *Yield: 2 dozen.*

Schuylkill County, a mining and farming area in Eastern Pennsylvania, was also Groundhog country. A local weekly paper, the *Citizen-Standard*, published at Valley View, occasionally mentions Groundhog hunting and eating. On April 24, 1992, an article entitled "A Good Recipe for Braised Woodchuck" appeared in the column "Appalachian Outdoor Meanderings," by outdoor writer Dick Wolff. It was sent in by Helen Wagner of Frackville.

Woodchuck should be skinned as you would a rabbit, being sure to remove the small kernel-like glands under the forelegs. Soak refrigerated overnight in salted water. Drain and wipe dry. Cut up. Dredge the pieces with seasoned flour. Melt in a skillet or Dutch oven three tablespoons butter. Saute the pieces in the butter until browned.

Cover thickly with sliced onions and pour 1½ cups dry red wine over all.

Cover and simmer one hour or place the pot in a 300 degree oven and bake until tender, about 1½ hours for a young woodchuck or a little longer for an older animal. Add more wine or water if necessary.

In 1975, a paperback, spiral-bound cookbook entitled *The Night Mayor from Kitchen to Parlor: Get to Know What Good Is!* was published by Carole Boehm of the Unitarian-Universalist Church of the historic Pennsylvania Dutch town of Reading, seat of Berks County. The book was dedicated to her late husband, Paul Barclay Boehm, Brooklyn native and adopted Berks Countian. As Paul Barclay, he hosted a radio show, the Night Mayor Program, which began in 1955 and ran for almost twenty

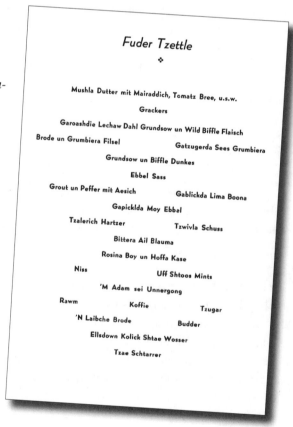

The 1935 menu of the second Fersommling of Groundhog Lodge Number One on the Lehigh includes Roast Lehigh County Groundhog and Groundhog Gravy.
ROUGHWOOD
COLLECTION

Fuder Tzettle

❖

Mushla Dutter mit Mairaddich, Tomatz Bree, u.s.w.

Grackers

Garoashdie Lechaw Dahl Grundsow un Wild Biffle Flaisch

Brode un Grumbiera Filsel

Gatzugerda Sees Grumbiera

Grundsow un Biffle Dunkes

Ebbel Sass

Grout un Peffer mit Aesich

Gablickda Lima Boona

Gapicklda Moy Ebbel

Tzalerich Hartzer

Tzwivla Schuss

Bittera Ail Blauma

Rosina Boy un Hoffa Kase

Niss

Uff Shtoos Mints

'M Adam sei Unnergong

Rawm

Koffie

Tzugar

'N Laibche Brode

Budder

Ellsdown Kolick Shtae Wosser

Tzae Schtarrer

years. What started out as a one-hour show became two hours in 1956, three in 1958, and four in 1972. This immensely popular program was a call-in show dealing with the widest possible range of interests that concerned Berks Countians, from local politics to health and food. Numerous recipes were swapped, a selection of which appears in the book. The recipe collection, which was put together by the church women, includes many Pennsylvania Dutch favorites, including squirrel stew for a crowd—made from seventy squirrels—pickled pigs' feet, pigs' feet jelly, German hot potato salad, pickled red beet eggs, dandelion dressing, Mohjy apples, and yes, Groundhog. The recipe follows:

> Soak a cleaned groundhog in salt water. Bring to a boil in clean water and boil for 5 minutes. Change water and cook until almost tender. Add onion, potato, celery and parsley. Cook until done.
>
> Or groundhog may be baked after second change of clear water.
>
> (We do not know anyone who has tried this recipe.)

An excellent collection of Groundhog recipes can be found in Trapper Jack French's *Pioneer Heritage Wild Game Cookbook* (1986). Trapper Jack says that the Groundhog's "naturally dark, fine grained meat is easy to become accustomed to, and makes a great tasting nutritious meal when it is properly prepared." It resembles beaver meat in flavor, he adds.

The following eight recipes he offers are varied and quite workable: "Country Baked Groundhog"; "Uncle Hub's Fried Groundhog"; "Trapper Jack's Groundhog Brunswick Stew," with potatoes, onions, lima beans, corn, okra, tomatoes, and lots of spices; "Groundhog Meatloaf"; "Grandmother's Groundhog Burgers"; "Frontiersman's Groundhog Pie"; "Uncle Dave's Groundhog Shish Kebab"; and "Trapper Jack's Famous Groundhog Soup," with dried lentils, onions, and rice. The author also points out that Groundhog can be substituted as the main ingredient in the squirrel and rabbit recipes in the book.

Two additional wild game cookbooks that include Groundhog recipes are Barbara Flood's *Game in the Kitchen: Cookery for Nimrods, Anglers, and Their Friends* (1968) and Jim Bryant's *The Wild Game and Fish Cookbook* (1984). Flood's book contains one recipe, "Groundhog (Whistle Pig) and Porcupine." She says, "both of these fat rascals are good eating," but the Groundhog is "not so difficult to clean as his first cousin, Porky, but that's your problem." The Groundhog is simmered in a marinade of vinegar and pickling spices, then roasted in orange juice seasoned with pepper and garlic salt. For the gourmet touch, Bryant offers an elaborate recipe for "Braised Groundhog and Bourbon Sauce," and a variant version with chili powder called "Mexicali Groundhog."

Here is a final tidbit from Philadelphia. Years ago, the *Philadelphia Inquirer* featured a columnist named John M. Cummings, who furnished many amusing and informative articles for the paper's metropolitan readership. A clipping in my files, undated but probably from the 1960s, is entitled "Steps to Take about Groundhog Roasting." This is how it begins:

> What would have happened if the groundhog, instead of returning to his snug underground nest, decided winter was over and it would be safe to roam the countryside after the fashion of his kind from time immemorial, as the saying goes? He might soon discover that many folks relish a ration of roast groundhog if properly prepared and served.
>
> Assume then, that you have a groundhog handy, that he has come to your kitchen fresh killed from his natural habit in the Quarryville country or 'way out west where Gobbler's Knob looks down on the good burghers of Punxsutawney. How would you prepare your groundhog or woodchuck for the oven?

Cummings then quotes the Punxsutawney *Cooking with the Groundhog* recipe, which he says was sent him by Helen Tannehill of Bryn Mawr— not part of Groundhog Country. After giving all the details as outlined in the cookbook, he ends with the following snide advice:

> Now you have the recipe right from the groundhog's mouth. For your information may we suggest that just as you finish your last cocktail, place the cooked groundhog on a wheelbarrow, take it to a remote section of your garden and in the presence of your guests bury it under four feet of earth and six inches of concrete. That'll keep the critter in his place and he'll never see his shadow again.
>
> Having performed this ceremony, reassemble your startled guests and march them to a good restaurant specializing in lobster.

CHAPTER VII

Groundhog Culture

As is natural for a local holiday custom gone national, the literature produced about Groundhog Day is extensive. It includes much amusing poetry and song, everything from doggerel to classic verse, spawned by the Groundhog Day organizations, clubs, and lodges. There is also an amazing spate of prose, especially charming children's books that have appeared in the last decades. And there is the widely popular Hollywood film, *Groundhog Day*, starring Bill Murray, which was discussed earlier.

Poems and songs in praise of the Groundhog, and of February 2, his day of prophecy, abound in Pennsylvania. They are in three languages: English, Pennsylvania Dutch, and Groundhogese, translated into English. Through many decades, local poets and poetasters have rivaled each other in producing them. They have been recited or sung, amid much hilarity, at the early Groundhog Club sessions at Punxsutawney, at the Slumbering Groundhog Lodge at Quarryville, and at all the current Pennsylvania Dutch Grundsow (Groundhog) Lodges of Eastern and Central Pennsylvania.

Some of these productions are anonymous, labeled simply "Inspired" or "By a Member"; others are signed. The early Punxsutawney verses were from the fluent pen of Clymer Freas. The Quarryville contingent of poets was led by Lancaster newspaperman Herman E. Hoch, who in 1908 was named Poet Laureate of the Slumbering Groundhog Lodge. In 1905 and 1906, he had produced two little plays in blank verse, entitled "The Groundhog's Prophecy." He was succeeded as Poet Laureate by H. B. Best. Other Quarryvillers who tried their hand at verse were J. Earl Newswanger, Charles G. Gochnauer, and the Elverson Bard.

Groundhog Day Poetry

In 1902, the prolific Clymer Freas, principal shaper of Punxsutawney's Groundhog Day celebration, was Poet Laureate and Supreme Secretary of the town's Groundhog Club, the earliest such institution in the nation. He wrote a poem entitled "Groundhog Club," which he recited at the fourth annual club banquet held on Groundhog Knob in September 1902. He repeated the performance before an audience of four hundred guests at the first Old Home Week Groundhog Banquet in 1909.

While the poem, as reported in the Punxsutawney *Spirit*, was intended to "roast" some of the club's prominent members, it does provide several titillating references to culinary Groundhogism. It praises the "woodchuck soup" that "beats bouillabaisse," gives a glimpse of the prophet "sizzling in hot grease," and includes the salivating mention of Groundhog hams and Groundhog broth.

Of the same vintage as the Freas poem is the lengthy "Groundhog Poem," by Herman C. Hoch, the talented early Poet Laureate of the Slumbering Groundhog Lodge of Quarryville. It has a classical rhythm and a mock heroic style that gives it permanent interest in the field of literary expressions of Groundhogism. Because of its length, only excerpts will be given here. It starts autobiographically with the words "I am a Prophet old, with forecasts manifold." It then goes back to Creation, "when stars together sang, while space with music rang, and worlds from chaos sprang." The earth now emerged from the "primeval storm" and took its shape in "spheric form." Finally man appears, and then:

> As age on age revolved
> Man gradually evolved,
> On higher aims resolved–
>   Grew less rapacious.
> Then, when a brighter age
> Illumined history's page,
> Appeared the groundhog sage,
>   Wise and sagacious.

Before the Fall of Troy, and Homer's epic:

On many a distant wold,
By classic rivers old,
Great groundhog seers had told
  Tidings prophetic.

Hoch's theme, that the Groundhog was ancient, prehistoric, primeval, was carried on by later poets. Another theme, that the Groundhog's prognostications are true, was sounded in another of Hoch's offerings:

Tell me, Oh! Mother Earth
In icy fetters bound
Is there no prophet true
In this world to be found?
No wizard, weather wise,
Whose bosom swells with truth,
Who never utters lies,
But always speaks the truth?
The cold world shook her chains from pole to pole
  And answered, Mortals, seek the groundhog's hole.

From the Punxsutawney *Spirit* for February 2, 1930, comes another theme common to this genre of literature, that one's Resident Groundhog, in this case Punxsutawney's, looks down on and derogates all other weather prognosticators as fakes. In verses entitled "I Am the One Great Forecaster," Punxsutawney's Groundhog boasts:

Oh, I am the Boss of the Weather;
I'm Monarch of heat and cold.
I'm all the great Seers put together.
And I'm more than a million years old.

The goose-bone, the big Weather Bureau,
The Quarryville pig—they are fakes,
On Candlemas Day they all fade away,
In the blaze of the Greatest of Snakes.

Then bow to your Lord and your Master,
And hell to the Sultan of Sleet,
For I am the one Great Forecaster;
The rest of them cringe at my feet.

Now hearken to me! Hear this my decree.
(Or by all the gods be accurst):
Hereafter, I say, your Candlemas Day
Shall happen on April the First!

Groundhog poetry often reflected current events, including the wars of the twentieth century. Most of the Pennsylvania Groundhog Lodges came through the Second World War period with flying colors. This Quarryville offering, "Patriotic Groundhogs on Duty," by Charles Francis Hess, brings memories of the war and hopes for a world at peace:

Though Atom bombs have rocked the world
And all now ponder what they herald,
The Groundhog comes to tell anew
A waiting world just what to do.

In times of peace, or time of war,
Unfailing, as he has before,
In second month, on second day
He asks no alms, exacts no pay.

But waking from this winter's sleep,
He ventures out to take a peep
And furnish us the news we lack–
The world's unfailing almanac.

For if the sun is bright o'erhead,
He quietly scurries back to bed.
Then all the faithful know once more
Six wintry weeks will blast their door.

But if he should no shadow see,
It's welcome news to you and me.
The farmer springs to life and toil,
He knows he soon can till the soil.

And as the ages come and go,
And if he brings us sun or snow,
Our hope is he will never cease
To look upon a world at peace.

Two more effusions, both inspired by the Quarryville muse, have a captivating rhythm and display the usual Groundhog mystique. The first of the two poems is simply called "Annual Poem by Lodge Poet" and is from the pen of the talented "Elverson Bard."

> As you journey on life's road with its ever-changing load—smiles and sorrows, joys and ills, and its valleys and its hills—pause as you go on your way, join in keeping Groundhog Day, help to celebrate the feast of the Prophets, not the least!
>
> Fact, he's greatest of them all, lean or stout, or short or tall! Any shape or any size, he's the wisest of the wise.
>
> In the spring-time (summer, too) when you've little else to do, you may see him in the fields gathering what Nature yields, rambling round and having fun, maybe basking in the sun.
>
> But when comes the chilly breeze whistling sharply through the trees, he retires beneath the ground where he rests in slumber sound (not a care upon his soul, income tax or lack of coal) gathering the facts together to forecast the future weather.
>
> Scientists all take back seat when the Groundhog does his feat. Groundhog knows just what to do. Renders information true. Doesn't resort to guessing tricks, goose-bones, woolyworm or Hicks. Naught for almanacs he cares—doesn't even look at Baer's and is quite suffused with smiles if is mentioned Dr. Miles.

This Groundhog jig is part of the annual ceremony at Quarryville. JAMES E. PENNINGTON COLLECTION

Then on the appointed day he comes forth and has his say. Gives
 his findings sane and sound to the waiting world around. Makes
 no charge, and asks no fee, all's as free as free can be.
Take your hat off to the Sage, greatest one of any age. Any age or time
 or place. He's the one who sets the pace.
Pause as you go on life's way, join in keeping Groundhog Day—most
 important date of all, summer, winter, spring or fall. Homage pay unto
 the Sage, Greatest Prophet of the age!

The second poem is entitled "High Larity."

Today the Ground Hog from his lair comes forth to seek a change of air
 and see about the weather. He sniffs the breeze, and looks around. He
 scans the sky and then the ground, and puts the facts together.
He wears no mortar board and gown. He doesn't even live in town, and
 never went to college. Was never sent away to school, and taught to
 live by rote or rule, or crammed with useless knowledge, but knows if
 fog obscures the sun, the course of winter has been run and spring will
 soon be here, and if the sun should shine to day springtime is full six
 weeks away, nor sooner will appear.
Perhaps some time the day may be, when folks are just as wise as he (but
 then Alas! Alack! how could we ever treat our ills, or take the proper
 liver pills without an Almanac). Now straightway to his dwelling go, and
 tossing high your best chapeau, give three resounding cheers, and let the
 public understand his like is not in all the land, nor has it been for years.

Dialect Poetry and Songs

The Pennsylvania Dutch muse has inspired reams of poetry, mostly classic
four-line verse with simple rhyme schemes. The themes include nostalgia
for the farm life one knew as a child, reminiscences of the food Mother
served on her bountiful table, ballads of past events in Pennsylvania Dutch
history, and somewhat fulsome praise of the Pennsylvania Dutch people
and their beloved mother tongue, *die Mudderschprooch*. A surprising number of the best nineteenth- and twentieth-century poets from the Dutch
Country have courted the muse to produce poems about the Groundhog
and his gift of weather prophecy.

One of the earliest poems to be written on the Groundhog as weather
prophet is a work called simply *"Die Grundsau"* ("The Groundhog"), by
Professor D. B. Brunner. It appears in a charming 1903 volume edited and

The LeRoy Heffentrager Band provides Pennsylvania Dutch oompah music for the Groundhog Lodges of the Lehigh Valley. CARL D. SNYDER COLLECTION

published by newspaperman Daniel Miller (1843–1913) of Reading, entitled *Pennsylvania German: A Collection of Pennsylvania German Productions in Poetry and Prose.* The poem contains twenty-six verses and thus is too long to reprint here. Professor Brunner, who was at the time a well-known Berks County school principal, did not think much of the Groundhog as weather prophet. He calls the whole Groundhog belief complex an example of human humbuggery. He likes the word *humbug* and uses it in Pennsylvania Dutch. In one of his verses, he declares that "the Groundhog doesn't know any more about the weather than an old jackass knows of a solar eclipse!" And that settles that.

John Birmelin (1873–1950), generally regarded as the outstanding Pennsylvania Dutch poet of the twentieth century, also wrote Groundhog poetry. Among his poems is *"Die Wedderbrophede,"* dealing with all the weather prophets, including the Washington Weatherman, the rooster crowing on the manure pile, the goose whose bones are "read" by goosebone prophets, and finally, the Groundhog. Another is *"Die Grundsau Kann's Net Verfehle"* ("The Groundhog Can't Miss It," in other words, can't be wrong about the weather). The title says it all.

When the Groundhog Lodge Movement got started in the 1930s, it was *de rigueur* for the Brother Groundhogs to sing songs in Dutch. The high point, or possibly the nadir, of this genre of dialect verse was reached with J. A. Angstadt's *"Grundsau, Grundsau, Iwwer Alles"* ("Groundhog, Groundhog, Over All"), a humorous takeoff on the old German national anthem and sung to that tune. Patsy Balliet's *"Oh die Alt Groh Grundsau"* ("Oh, the Old Gray Groundhog") and John Birmelin's *"Grundsau-Lied"* ("Groundhog Song"), sung to the German tune *"Im Wald und auf der Heide,"* are still circulating among the lodges, reprinted in many of their annual programs and sung merrily by hundreds of Brother Groundhogs before and after their copious Dutch banquets. Several songs were written by Montgomery Countian Henry C. Detweiler, whose *"Die Brofatzeihing"* ("The Prophesying"), sung to the tune "She'll Be Comin' Round the Mountain," is a popular item at many current Groundhog Lodges, as is his "Oh du Grundsau," to the tune of "Oh Susanna":

Do iss en schee Fersammeling,	This is a fine assembly–
Do hocka mir all rum,	Where we all sit around together.
All Pennsylfawnisch Deitscha Leit,	All Pennsylvania Dutch folk,
Mir gucka net so dumm!	We don't look so dumb!
Mir hen en neia Grundsau Lodge,	We have a new Groundhog Lodge,
Mir wissa aa ferwas.	We know the reason why.
Mir macha net en langes Gsicht,	We don't make long faces,
Mir gleicha wennich Gschpass.	We like a little fun!
Chorus	*Chorus*
Oh, Du Grundsau,	Oh, you Groundhog,
Du bischt unser Brofeet.	You are our Prophet.
Du seegscht uns was es Wedder gebt,	You tell us what the weather will be,
Ebs reggert oder schneet.	Whether it will rain or snow.
Der Weddermann iss net fiel wart,	The weather man isn't worth much,
Fum Wedder weess er nix.	Of the weather he knows nothing!
Wann mir uscht uff ihn harricha daet,	If we would just listen to him
Dann waer mir in ra Fix!	Then we'd really be in a fix!
Mir wissa was die Grundsau seecht,	We know what the Groundhog says,
Un was ass sie bericht.	And what it does report.
Mir halta sie in grosse Ehr,	We hold him in high honor,
Ferfehle dutt sie nicht.	Because he never fails!

Groundhog Day Songs and Carols

Among the rapidly burgeoning Groundhog Day literature spreading over the country from the various Groundhog Day centers are songs about Groundhog Day. The rousing "February Second," sung to the tune of "John Brown's Body," is from the Quarryville Slumbering Groundhog Lodge. Picture the worthies attired in their long white nightshirts and their formal top hats, singing every verse lustily, and giving each chorus a thundering éclat.

Let the scientific fakirs gnash their teeth and stomp with rage—
Let astrologers with crystals wipe such nonsense from the page—
We hail the King of Prophets, who's the world's outstanding Sage—
                Today the Groundhog comes!

Let the makers of the almanac from Dr. Miles to Hicks—
Let the goosebones and the woolyworms resort to all their tricks—
Let the Bureau of the Weather do its part by throwing bricks—
                Today the Groundhog comes!

And while his human neighbors have to guess when the winter goes,
The Groundhog with his triflin' labor, measures, calculates and knows
If spring will soon be with us, or we'll still have ice and snows—
                Today the Groundhog comes!

His findings are most accurate, authentic and exact,
On February (second day) he states the simple fact
And none from his decision can a single point detract—
                Today the Groundhog comes!

Chorus
Glory! Glory! to the Groundhog,
Glory! Glory! to the Groundhog,
Glory! Glory! to the Groundhog,
Today the Prophet comes!

Three Groundhog songs appeared in the Sun Prairie, Wisconsin, pamphlet *Celebrate! February 2nd,* issued by the Sun Prairie Chamber of Commerce.

"Groundhog Day"
To the tune of "Dashing Thru the Snow"

He sleeps in the ground
On a farm outside of town
His little ears are round
And his coat is furry brown
The same time every year
February second is the day
That we find out if Spring is near
Or Winter's here to stay . . .

Chorus
To the tune of "Jingle Bells"

Groundhog Day
Groundhog Day
Jimmy wakes today
To tell the folks
Around the world
What his shadow had to say . . .

"Jimmy, the Little Brown Groundhog"
To the tune of "Rudolph the Red-Nosed Reindeer"

Jimmy, the little brown groundhog
Lives on a farm near Sun Prairie
And through the long cold winter
He sleeps so very peacefully
Then on February second
Jimmy opens up an eye
And if he sees his shadow
We all shake our heads and sigh
If Jimmy sees his shadow then
We know that winter will stay
But if the sky is dark and gray
We know that spring is on its way
Jimmy the little brown groundhog
Has done his little task again
And we who love Sun Prairie
Share our fun and joy with him!

Jimmy the Groundhog of Sun Prairie, Wisconsin, caught in a relaxed mood, possibly listening to Groundhog Day carols. SUN PRAIRIE CHAMBER OF COMMERCE

"Jimmy, the 8th, Groundhog"
To the tune of "I'm Henry the 8th"

I'm Jimmy the 8th, I am,
Jimmy the 8th, I am, I am
I'm related to the Jimmys before.
There's been 7 other hogs before.
And every one was a Jimmy, Jimmy!
It couldn't be a Willy or a Phil. Or a Phil!
I'm the 8th old hog, I'm Jimmy
Jimmy the 8th I am.

The most winsome of all the songs produced in honor of the Ground-hog and Groundhog Day are those in the little collection of thirty items entitled *Groundhog Day Carols: A Selection of Songs by John and Jan Haigis Celebrating This Special Time of Year,* published in 1997 by the Mar-velous Megalethoscope at St. Peter's Village in Chester County. John and Jan Haigis are a husband and wife team, both teachers, singers, songwriters, musicians, and historians. Their carol booklet is accompanied by a cassette

The cover of Groundhog Day Carols, *a collection of clever parodies of familiar yuletide numbers, published in 1997.*
JOHN AND JAN HAIGIS

containing the sung versions of twenty-four of their songs, and in addition they have issued music tapes called "Carousel Horses" and "A Child's Garden of Song," based on the poems of Robert Louis Stevenson. In their booklet, they explain what inspired them to write Groundhog Day carols:

> Several years ago, we had an opportunity to play Santa and Mrs. Claus on Philadelphia's South Street. We enjoyed singing the songs of the season, but abruptly the season was over; so we asked ourselves: "OK, What's the next big holiday?" "Groundhog Day, of course." "What songs are there for that?" "Me and My Shadow, that's about it." Now, through the wonders of sleep deprivation and the disease of "Groundhoghaigisitis," we present these songs celebrating this special time of year. . . . Yea Spring!!!!!

"Punxsutawney Phil Looked Out"
To the tune of "Good King Wenceslas"

Punxsutawney Phil looked out
From his winter dwelling,
Saw no shadow on the ground,
Springtime was foretelling.

Winter soon will go away,
Warmth of spring returning,
Longer now gets every day,
As the planet's turning.

Winter winds are icy cold,
A chilly type sensation,
So that we resort to find,
Some warmth in hibernation.
Snug within our burrows,
We escape the winter's blast,
Till in good time we shall see
Spring return at last.

"Heating Bills"
To the tune of "Jingle Bells"

A month or two ago,
The snow began to fall,
The temperature went down,
And I went up the wall.
The furnace started in
To fight the winter's chill,
And everything was fine until
I got my heating bill.

Heating bills, Heating bills,
Soon will go away.
Oh, how we look forward to
The word on Groundhog Day.
Heating bills, Heating bills
Soon will all be gone.
Oh, how much we miss the sight
Of flowers on the lawn!

"Good Groundhogs now Rejoice"
To the tune of "Good Christian Men"

Good Groundhogs now rejoice,
But don't make any noise.
Listen now to what we say,

Winter soon will go away,
Warmth of Spring will soon be found,
We see no shadow on the ground.
Spring will soon be here.
Spring will soon be here!

"Hark How He Tells"
To the tune of "Carol of the Bells"

Hark how he tells; see how he smells,
Sniffing the air, out from his lair,
Poking about, raising his snout,
Forecasting spring, making us sing.
In Punxsutawney, greeting the dawn, he
Stands in the light of observers' sight.
Will the groundhog see his shadow?
Will the groundhog see his shadow?

"Check the Calls"
To the tune of "Deck the Halls"

Check the calls to Punxsutawney,
Following the winter comes the spring.
Wanting now to mow the lawn, we
Watch prognostication's famous king.
(If the groundhog sees his shadow,
Winter will be hanging on for six weeks more!)
Ready for the warmth of springtime,
Ready to shove winter out the door!

"I Heard the Word from Gobbler's Knob"
To the tune of "It Came upon a Midnight Clear"

I heard the word from Gobbler's Knob,
The call came loud and clear.
How spring would soon spread its joyful warmth,
'Cause no shadow did appear!

When Phil did out of the ground emerge
And looked on a winter scene,
We knew that as the year goes on
The land would soon be green.

"Everywhere You Look"
To the tune of "Short'nin Bread"

Everywhere you look
You see a groundhog, groundhog,
Everybody celebrates
On Groundhog Day.

Up in the morning,
What does he see?
A shadow means there's
Six more weeks of
Winter's freeze.

But if in the morning,
No shadow is seen
Springtime round the corner
Is what that means.

Everywhere you look
You see a groundhog, groundhog
Everybody celebrates
On Groundhog Day.

"Groundhog Peers from Burrow of Brown"
To the tune of "We Three Kings"

Groundhog peers from burrow of brown,
Lifts his head, and looks around,
Sees his shadow, somewhat sad-o,
Six more weeks underground!
Oh, time of winter, time of cold,
Long, long nights, it gets real old.
Sleeting, sneezing, sniffling, freezing,
Winter joys which we behold.

"Groundhog Saw No Shadow"
To the tune of "Joshua Fought the Battle of Jericho"

Groundhog saw no shadow on the frozen ground,
Frozen ground, frozen ground.
Groundhog saw no shadow on the frozen ground,
And the spring it soon came round.

You may talk about your signs and portents,
And prognostications by the way.
But there's nothing like that old Groundhog,
And the word on Groundhog Day.

Groundhog saw no shadow on the frozen ground,
Frozen ground, frozen ground.
Groundhog saw no shadow on the frozen ground,
And the spring it soon came round.

A Sheaf of Children's Books

In researching the long and complicated history of Groundhog Day in the United States, one thing that surprised me was the large number of recent children's books on the Groundhog and Groundhog Day—several dozen, in fact. Many of these books can usually be found in the children's sections of local public libraries. At my nearest local library, the Tredyffrin Township Library, I found six of them in the catalogue. One was checked out, but I read with great amusement the five that were on the shelves.

The first of these was *Gretchen Groundhog, It's Your Day!* (1978) by Abby Levine and illustrated by Nancy Cote. The story line involves the shy Gretchen Groundhog, who, when her great-uncle Gus got too old, took over the job of going through the rigmarole of February 2. The book has many amusing touches, such as naming Gertrude's hometown Piccadilly, undoubtedly a spinoff of Punxsutawney. Gertrude's family history is presented in detail, starting with Goody Groundhog, who came over on the Mayflower; George Groundhog, who was at Valley Forge with Washington; General Grant Groundhog, of Civil War renown; and Gloria Groundhog, the movie star. And the book gets the history of Groundhog Day right, saying that "German pioneers in Pennsylvania transferred the belief to the groundhog."

Another offering is *It's Groundhog Day!* (1987) by Steven Kroll and illustrated by Jeni Bassett. This book features Godfrey Groundhog and his friends Roland Raccoon, Penelope Porcupine, Reginald Rabbit, and others. All fall, Godfrey eats and eats to get ready for hibernation, then sleeps through Christmas and New Year's. On February 2, Roland Raccoon kidnaps Godfrey and puts him in a bag so he won't see his shadow. But the wily Godfrey escapes and doesn't see his shadow anyway—it's too cloudy.

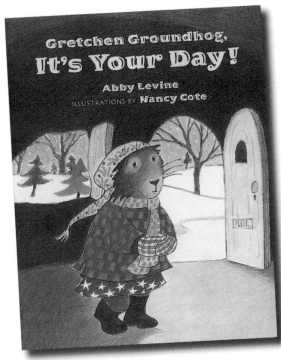

Gretchen Groundhog prepares to leave for her tour of duty on the cover of the popular children's book. ALBERT WHITMAN AND COMPANY

In *Geoffrey Groundhog Predicts the Weather* (1995), by Bruce Koscielniak, Geoffrey is a resident of Mooseflats in Mooseflats County, and his adventures are covered by Merton Moose, editor of the local newspaper. On February 2, alas, Geoffrey oversleeps and arrives on the scene late. With all the cameras and lights, he isn't sure if he sees his shadow, suffering, it seems, from "Groundhog Daze." Finally, he does see his shadow and predicts six more weeks of winter. The book has many clever features, including a takeoff on the commercialization that today surrounds Groundhog Day. Geoffrey's picture is used on many products, such as Ground Hoggers Jogging Shoes, Geoffrey Groundhog Sunglasses, and Big Tooth Tooth Paste, and a local restaurant advertises that "Geoffrey Ate Here."

Marvin Glass's *What Happened Today, Freddy Groundhog?* (1989) is memorable, among other things, for Freddy's byword, "Wigglin' Woodchucks!" and for interesting cutaway drawings of Freddy's burrow.

In addition, the Punxsutawney story is featured in three books by Julia Spencer Moutran: *Story of Punxsutawney Phil, the Fearless Forecaster* (1987); *Will Spring Ever Come to Gobbler's Knob?* (1992); and *Punxsutawney Phil and His Weather Wisdom* (1997). Barbara Birenbaum has contributed four Groundhog books in all: *Hidden Shadow* (1986); *Ground-hog Message* (2000); *Groundhog Willie's Shadow* (2001); and *Groundhog Phil's Message: Groundhog Legends and Lore* (2002). Among the other children's books devoted to the Groundhog are Judy Cox's *Go to Sleep, Groundhog* (2003); Susan Korman's *Wake Up, Groundhog!* (1997); Janet McDonnell's *Winter Tracks in the Snow* (1993); Kate McMullan's *Fluffy Meets the Groundhog* (2001); Jean Warren's *Huff and Puff on Groundhog Day* (1995); and Peter J. Welling's *Andrew McGroundhog and his Shady Shadow* (2001). Each of these books is charmingly illustrated by either the author or a talented specialist in presenting ideas to children.

This genre of children's literature, featuring humanized animals living underground in snug, comfortable quarters—always attractive to children, with their playhouse mentality—resembles A. A. Milne's *Winnie the Pooh* series. And like the Pooh characters, these fictional Groundhogs come very close to being animal toys.

With the humanizing of the Groundhog in all these intriguing stories, let's hope that they not only amuse children, but also help teach them the central place of animal life in Mother Nature's realm. Let's have more such charming children's books!

Through the centuries, some of the most popular festivals have gradu-ally metamorphosed to revolve around children's activities. In the Middle Ages, holidays were celebrated by adults in European society. It was grownups who masked and reveled and feasted and danced on key days in the celebratory year, such as Christmas, New Year's, and Mardi Gras. But some holidays have become either partially or wholly children's festivals.

The best example is Halloween, which is now chiefly celebrated by trick-or-treating children. Christmas and Easter are more complex, but both also largely involve children. With this great wave of children's books on the market, it is possible that Groundhog Day is coming to appeal more and more to children. Teenagers, at least those of college age, can also be aficionados of the Groundhog Day mystique, as evidenced by the great numbers of college students reveling in the festivities on Gobbler's Knob. But adults—the top-hatted Inner Circle, the nightshirted Slumber-ing Groundhog Lodge, and the hundreds of Pennsylvania Dutchmen who attend the Groundhog Lodges each year, with all their tongue-in-cheek ritualism and Brother Groundhogging—undoubtedly are still the leading component of the festival.

CHAPTER VIII

Other Weather Lore

B esides Groundhog Day, there were other weather-predicting days in the Pennsylvania Dutch folk calendar that were brought from Europe. A runner-up to Groundhog Day is July 2, when, as all Upstate Pennsylvanians know, "Mary goes over the mountain." In addition there are St. Swithin's Day (July 15), a folkloric implant from the British Isles, and Rain Day (July 29) in Waynesburg, Greene County, Pennsylvania.

Mary Goes over the Mountain

On July 2, according to the ancient saying, "Mary goes over the mountain." The mountain is never specified. Just as in connection with Groundhog Day, there is a long and complex background to this belief, and both days are connected to medieval Catholic ideas about the Virgin Mary.

In the Middle Ages, the Roman Catholic Church developed a series of Marian festivals in the Church calendar, days dedicated to and honoring St. Mary. July 2 was called the Festival of the Visitation of Mary, or in German: *Mariä-Heimsuchung*. According to the Gospel of St. Luke, 1:39–56, Mary paid a formal visit to her cousin Elizabeth, mother of John the Baptist, to impart to her the news of the Annunciation, the Angel Gabriel's announcement to Mary that she would miraculously bear a child named

Jesus. In the fourth century, when December 25 was set as the date to commemorate the birthday of Jesus, the Church fathers set the date of the Annunciation artificially at March 25–exactly nine months before the birth.

In South German and Austrian folklore, March 25 is called *Schwalbentag*, the Day of the Swallows. A folk rhyme explains why:

> When Gabriel does the message bring,
> Return the swallows, comes the spring.

Another folk rhyme connects the weather and the season to the day in this way:

> Saint Gabriel to Mary flies:
> This is the end of snow and ice.

The whole legend is recapped in a children's song sung on September 8, the day set by the Church as Mary's birthday:

> It's Blessed Virgin's Birthday,
> The swallows do depart;
> Far to the South they fly away,
> And sadness fills my heart.
> But after snow and ice and rain
> They will in March return again.

Thus all of these Marian holidays were considered weather days. On September 8, the swallows fly south, symbolic of the coming of winter, and on March 25 they return, heralding the arrival of spring.

The medieval cycle of Church festivals devoted to the Virgin Mary forms the official-religious underpinning of the folk-religious concept of "Mary goes over the mountain." The Protestant Pennsylvania Dutch farmers forgot most of the day's medieval religious significance and treated July 2 simply as a weather day. All they remembered was that Mary was involved, and that she went somewhere on that day. So in the folk version of the belief, Mary leaves ("goes over the mountain") on July 2 and returns on August 15, six weeks later. August 15 is another Marian feast day on the Church calendar, commemorating the belief in her Assumption into heaven.

The common people were divided on how July 2 determined the weather. One version was that if it rains when she leaves (July 2), it will be dry when she returns (August 15), and vice versa. The second version is that if it rains the day she leaves, it will rain for six weeks; but if July 2 is dry, there will be six weeks of dry weather. Mark Trumbore of Montgomery County recorded a somewhat vulgar Dutch saying about all this: *"Wann sie net brunst wann sie geht, dann brunst sie wann sie kummt,"* "If she doesn't urinate when she goes, she urinates when she comes."

A valuable reference to the awe in which July 2 was held by farmers appears in an 1887 Virginia novel set at the beginning of the Civil War, *Behind the Blue Ridge*, by Frances C. Baylor:

> The second of July is a noted day in the Mountain calendar always, and was marked by a special event this year, remembered and recalled for many a year after. It is known as "the day the Virgin Mary takes her visit," and if any inquirer, surprised to find this curious bit of Catholic mosaic inserted in a stony and colorless stretch of Protestant pavement, asks anything more about it, he is told that it is "a sign,"—usually, "my father's sign," or "my grandfather's sign," to give it the supreme stamp of authority. It is then explained that if it rains on that day the crops are sure to be as satisfactory as crops ever are to the farmer; and that if it does not rain on that day a six weeks' drought may be looked for, since not a drop will the heavens vouchsafe until "the Lady returns back to her own home." This being the case, it was natural that in an agricultural community in which this unpoetical version of the Visitation was generally accepted the day that gave good or poor crops was anxiously expected before it arrived and inspected when it came. But this year it was actually a matter of secondary interest, for the axe had fallen, the die had been cast, Virginia had seceded, and this was also the day set for "the soldiers (by brevet) to go to the war."

St. Swithin's Day

July 15 is a prominent weather day in British Isles folklore known as St. Swithin's Day. Swithin was a ninth-century monk-priest whose life story attracted numerous legends. Swithin died on July 2, in the year 862, but the weather lore associated with him is observed on July 15, the date when his bones were transferred in 1093 to the new Winchester Cathedral in southern England. He became a weather saint willy-nilly, and as the rhyme about him goes:

St. Swithin's Day if thou dost rain,
For forty days it will remain;
St. Swithin's Day if thou be fair,
For forty days 'twill rain na mair.

In 1538, as part of the Protestant campaign to remove superstition from the new Anglican Church, Henry VIII ordered the shrine at Winchester destroyed. A new one was erected years ago and was dedicated on July 15, 1962.

In Pennsylvania, according to the late Prof. Mac E. Barrick, who collected folklore in Cumberland and adjoining counties of Central Pennsylvania, west of Harrisburg, "if it rains on St. Swithin's Day (July 15), it will rain for forty days," and "if St. Swithin's Day comes on a Sunday and it rains, it'll rain for seven more Sundays."

Rain Day in Waynesburg

In Waynesburg, seat of Greene County and center of a farming region in the far southwestern corner of Pennsylvania, another weather-predicting event is celebrated each year on July 29. According to an article by Janet Hodel, Rain Day has been celebrated there since 1939, with roots that go back much further. Because of their great dependence on rain, farmers in Europe and America have used three methods to bring rain when there has been a dry spell. The magical method involves imitative magic, such as pouring water from a treetop to encourage rain, beating drums to encourage thunder, or waving firebrands to imitate lightning. The religious method involves sacrifice and prayer to influence God to send rain. The scientific method uses natural means to alter nature's course.

Rain Day got its start in Waynesburg one day in 1879 at the town's central drugstore, a popular gathering place for the townsfolk. Two brothers, William and Albert Allison, were the clerks. One day a farmer shopping at the store remarked to William that it always seemed to rain on July 29. William jotted this down in his daybook and determined to check it out. His brother Albert recorded what happened each year on that date and invited local townsmen to an all-night vigil around a keg of beer as they waited for the raindrops. One of the crowd customarily made a bet that no rain would arrive, and if he lost, he paid for the beer.

Byron Daily, keeper of the Rain Day records, in his drug store in Waynesburg.
ROUGHWOOD COLLECTION

In the 1920s, the recording of the weather action was taken over by Byron Daily, the new proprietor of the drugstore. He added the further touch in 1927 of wagering hats with the traveling salesmen from the drug companies. Daily lost only twice, in 1930 and again in 1937.

With Byron Daily's death in 1938, the title of Rain Prophet was passed on to his son John, an attorney. A local newspaperman, John O'Hara, joined forces with John Daily in contacting celebrities to place bets. Among them were Jack Dempsey (1946), Bing Crosby (1947), Bob Hope (1948), Cassius Clay (1963), and Arnold Palmer (1964). In 1966, Punxsutawney's National Groundhog Club was chosen as that year's celebrity. The club made John Daily a life member.

Of the ninety-six years in which records were kept, up to 1975, it rained in Waynesburg eighty-three times. Pennsylvania meteorologists explain this curious fact by pointing out that the topography of the Waynesburg area is what makes it likely to rain in the town around July 29.

Throughout the years, there has been no official attempt to commercialize the event, although certain Rain Day customs evolved. In the 1930s, the county courthouse bell tolled when rain appeared; later, the town fire siren sounded. A local bank awarded a $25 savings certificate to the person who came closest to guessing the time the rain would start. Persons not carrying umbrellas were fined, and merchants were awarded prizes for the best holiday window decor. To Daily and O'Hara's dismay the event became a carnival, complete with a queen and an Indian rain dance.

In an attempt to avoid too garish a carnival atmosphere, in 1973 the Waynesburg Rain Day and Folklore Association was organized. Working with the county historical society and local folklore groups, the association functioned to keep the holiday tied to its original significance and prevent its commercialization for personal profit.

To help steer the celebration of the holiday, in 1979 the Waynesburg Borough Special Events Commission was initiated. Since then, the commission has sponsored an annual street fair in the town's center. Live entertainers perform all day on the courthouse steps, and thousands of visitors patronize the food stands, arts and crafts booths, children's game areas, and other amusements. At 5 P.M., there is a moment of silence to pay tribute to the many Waynesburg soldiers who were casualties during World War I on Rain Day, when nearly half of the 250 Greene County men then serving in France were either killed or wounded. Each Rain Day since 1979 has also featured a Miss Rain Day Pageant, a beauty contest for local teenagers, with the lucky winner awarded a crown and scholarship money.

Through its annual Rain Day celebration, little Waynesburg has achieved widespread recognition as a weather town. Each year, media from across the United States, and even other countries, including England, Australia, Japan, and Ethiopia, call the town of Waynesburg on July 29 to find out if it has rained.

On the Pennsylvania Dutch traditional calendar, June 29, one month before Waynesburg's Rain Day, was *Peter und Paul*, St. Peter and Paul's Day. Dutch farmers had a little rhyme, *"Peter und Paul macht die Wurzel faul,"* "Peter and Paul makes the root crops rot," meaning that it usually rained on June 29 as well.

My ancient Pennsylvania almanac in the German language calls July 29 *St. Beatrix*, St. Beatrice's Day. I don't know her connection, if any, with the weather, but in this almanac in the column headed *"Muthmassliche Witterung für Jeden Tag,"* "Probable Weather for Each Day," July 28 and 29 are marked *"trübe"* ("overcast"), and July 30 and 31 *"helle"* ("clear"), so perhaps there is something to it after all.

St. Mary of the Snows

A fascinating bit of Pennsylvania Dutch weather lore, also connected with the Virgin Mary, is the name given by Upstate Dutchmen to August 5: *Maria Schnee,* the Snow of St. Mary. I had always been intrigued by this folk designation for the day, and some years ago I assigned it as a research topic to my excellent student Hilda Adam Kring to work on in connection with my course in folk religion at the University of Pennsylvania.

The legend, of which the Dutch preserved only the name, is purported to have taken place in Rome, then the capital of Christendom, during the pontificate of Pope Liberius, 352–366 A.D. An ancient chronicle tells the story of John the Patrician and his wife, a childless couple in Rome, who wished to give their fortune to the church. One night both they and the pope had the same miraculous dream, in which the Virgin Mary proclaimed that where they found snow in Rome on August 5, they were to erect a

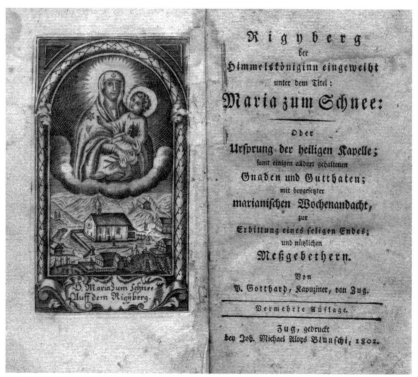

A Swiss pilgrimage book with prayers and devotions to St. Mary of the Snows on Mount Rigi, 1802. ROUGHWOOD COLLECTION

church. It snowed that day on the Esquiline Hill, and exactly where the miraculous snow fell, the basilica of *Santa Maria Maggiore*, St. Mary Major, was built, one of Rome's four basilicas or leading churches to this day.

"Our Lady of the Snows" became a favorite title of St. Mary in Italian folklore, and the cult spread northward to Germany, Switzerland, and elsewhere in Central Europe. From Germany and Switzerland, the name *Maria Schnee* for August 5 was brought to Pennsylvania by the Colonial immigrants. Although relatively rare today, the term can still be heard among elderly Pennsylvania Dutchmen.

As an example of the spread of the cult of St. Mary of the Snows north of the Alps into Switzerland, reproduced on the previous page are the frontispiece and title page from a little pilgrimage volume entitled *Rigyberg der Himmelsköniginn eingeweiht unter dem Titel: Maria zum Schnee* ("Mount Rigi, Consecrated to the Queen of Heaven under the Title: St. Mary of the Snows"), published at Zug in Catholic Switzerland in 1802. The frontispiece shows the Virgin Mary and her child above the Chapel of St. Mary of the Snows, on the Rigi, one of Central Switzerland's mountains of pilgrimage. It is often snow-covered and is sought out by both religious pilgrims and modern tourists, who, if really adventurous, make the trip up the mountain, now by train, to watch the sunrise from the mountain's heights.

More Weather Signs

In an 1891 article entitled "Folk-Lore from Buffalo Valley, Central Pennsylvania," J. G. Owens of Lewisburg, Union County, gives several weather signs gathered from the Pennsylvania Dutch. Most of his sources were over the age of seventy, some even ninety years or more.

One method of predicting a mild or severe winter was to examine the ears of corn at harvest time. If the ears had burst open or projected beyond the husks, this meant a mild winter; if the ears were plump and tightly encased in the husk, a severe winter was expected.

The farmers also watched their poultry and animals as weather predictors. When the ground was covered with snow, if the turkeys went into the fields or the guineas were heard making their curious cries, a thaw was forecast. If chickens sought shelter from a rainstorm, this meant it would not last long. On the other hand, if chickens walking about in the rain had their tail feathers down, it would continue to rain until they raised them. Hogs also were considered barometers. If they began to fight among themselves, a storm was portended. One farmer, from White Deer Valley, told Owens he kept a small herd of hogs feeding in the nearby mountains for several months each fall. One evening, they all hurried into the barnyard and began gathering straw to make nests. That night, a very heavy snow fell that lasted through the winter.

In the Buffalo Valley, the leech, used to bleed patients in earlier medical practice, was also employed in a strange method of weather prediction. In haymaking time in the summer, Owens writes, it would be especially convenient to find out what the weather will be at least a day ahead. Local farmers would go to a stream and catch a leech, placing it in a glass jar four-fifths full with at least a quart of water. The jar was closed with a linen strip and placed on the windowsill. Then the farmer watched the leech's motions very carefully to forecast the next day's weather. If the leech lay on the bottom in a circle, without moving, this meant the weather would be fine and clear. If it was going to rain, the leech would crawl to the top and remain there until the rain began. If windy, the leech would run around till the wind stopped. If thundershowers and heavy rains were coming, the leech would get out of the water, and twist and stretch as if it were in pain. This prognostication let the farmer and his hands know whether to hurry up with the haymaking that day, or whether they could finish it the next. Evidently the prophetic leech could predict the weather in winter as well as summer:

> During great cold in winter and great heat in summer it will lie still on the bottom. If there is to be snow or damp and rainy weather, it will fasten itself up at the mouth of the jar. In summer give it fresh water every week at least, and in winter every two weeks. With this care it will live for years, and cost only a little trouble.

The most thorough student of Pennsylvania Dutch weather lore was Dr. Edwin Miller Fogel (1874–1949), professor of Germanic languages and literatures at the University of Pennsylvania. A student of Dr. Marion Dexter Learned (1857–1918), dean of Pennsylvania Dutch research scholarship in the first decades of the twentieth century, Fogel was Learned's associate in editing and publishing the series *Americana Germanica* and succeeded him at the university. One of the principal founders of the Pennsylvania German Folklore Society in 1935, Dr. Fogel had grown up in Dutch-speaking Lehigh County. For his 1915 compendium of folkloric materials, *Beliefs and Superstitions of the Pennsylvania Germans,* he traveled widely through the Dutch counties of Eastern and Central Pennsylvania, interviewing speakers of the dialect and recording their lore. From his research travels abroad, he added relevant parallels from the traditional lore of Germany and the British Isles. His book includes many items on Groundhog Day and other aspects of Pennsylvania Dutch weather lore, of which the following is a sampling:

To predict the number of snows in the winter, there were several methods. One could count the number of days from the first snow to the next following full moon or to the end of the month, and that would be the number of snows that would fall that winter. Alternatively, the day of the month of the first snowstorm would indicate the number of snows that would fall during the winter.

Rain on religious holidays foretold more rain. Rain on Whitsunday, or Pentecost, fifty days after Easter, would be followed by seven rainy Sundays. If rain occurred on Good Friday, this meant seven rainy Sundays to follow, as well as high winds and a poor hay crop that summer. If it rained on John Huss Day, July 6, the celebration of the pre-Protestant martyr burned at the stake in 1415, the nut crop would be poor. Cumulus clouds on Jacob's Day, July 25, meant deep snow that winter. If the weather was fine on All Saints' and All Souls' Days, November 1 and 2, there would be six more weeks of fine weather; if it was cold and raw, winter was at hand.

Fogel also included a number of weather predictors from the animal world. If owls hooted from the hills, it indicated clear weather; if from pine trees, disagreeable weather. And if they hooted at nightfall or after daybreak, it also meant bad weather. If wild geese flew high in the air, it indicated warm weather; if they flew near the ground, it would be cold. When old women displayed their nightcaps (spiderwebs were meant), rain could be expected. Webs on the grass were generally also a sign of rain. If caterpillars were seen late in fall, the winter would be mild.

There were many other signs from nature. If the tops of trees were bare while the sides were still covered with leaves, the winter would be mild; if the leaves fell from the sides first, the winter would be severe. The length of icicles between Christmas and New Year indicated the depth of the snow during the winter. Long icicles before New Year predicted long flax the next year. Others believed the length of icicles on Shrove Tuesday, or Mardi Gras, the eve of Lent, indicated the height the flax would reach.

The moon was often observed for weather prognostication. If the horns of the moon were turned downward, it was a sign of rain. When the Indian could hang his powder horn on the moon, meaning that the horns were turned upward, the weather would be clear. A circle around the moon indicated rain, and the number of stars inside the circle denoted the number of days until it would rain.

Pains sensed in the body were also considered tokens of rain, and if a clock with brass works ticked very loudly it was considered a sign of stormy weather.

That they were so highly conscious of changes in the weather and observed such a great variety of signs to make predictions shows how important the weather was to the Pennsylvania Dutch farm folk of past generations, especially in the nineteenth century. The calendar was an important framework, and the natural world had many predictors as well.

American Science Looks at Weather Lore

In the 1880s, American government officials began to conduct research into the folklore of weather conditions. Gen. William Babcock Hazen (1830–87), then the chief signal officer of the U.S. War Department, proposed a collection of the "popular weather proverbs and prognostics used throughout the country." To gather this information, he issued a circular requesting popular weather sayings to be classified in the following categories:

> Proverbs relating to (1) the sun, (2) the moon, (3) stars and meteors, (4) rainbows, (5) mist and fog, (6) dew, (7) clouds, (8) frost, (9) snow, (10) rain, (11) thunder and lightning, (12) winds, (13) prognostics from the actions of animals, (14) from birds, (15) fish, (16) reptiles, (17) insects, (18) trees, plants, etc., (19) prognostics of the weather drawn from various objects [this included a great variety of portents, such as those derived from chairs, tables cracked before rain, coals, candles, lamps, smoke, corns, and rheumatism], (20) proverbs relating to days of the week, (21) months of the year, (22) seasons of the year, (23) the year, (24) all proverbs of weather and popular sayings not included under the above heads.

Obviously the Groundhog lore would be included in such a research network. Reviewing the project in an 1889 article called "Weather-Lore," in the *Journal of American Folk-Lore,* Fanny D. Bergen and W. W. Newell stated that the monograph that issued from the questionnaires was unfortunately, not competently presented, since "the localities in which the proverbs were current were not indicated" and copious British and European proverbial lore was added, so that the reader was at a loss to determine "how much in the collection was really American."

So pioneer folklorists Bergen and Newell issued their own collection of weather lore, prefaced with the following attribution of most of America's weather lore from British Isles sources:

> American weather-lore is chiefly derived from English lore, which again is only a part of the common stock of western and central Europe. A discussion of some of these proverbs would require elaborate articles, and involve inquiry into the calendar and religious festivals of ancient nations, both European and Asiatic. Some of these sayings may receive investigation hereafter; but for the present, we confine ourselves to printing a few examples of American proverbs, some of which are matched by corresponding English saws, while others are not exactly paralleled in British collections.

Other weather predicting days are cited in the diary of James L. Morris of Morgantown, Berks County. Under date of December 22, 1845, he wrote:

> The 20th, 21st and 22nd of this month used to be and perhaps still are observed by the old Germans as a means of knowing what kind of weather we shall have for the three succeeding months, for as these days are, in temperature, so shall the weather, or more especially the wind, be for 3 months.

Quaker Rejection of Weather Lore

The nineteenth-century Quaker poet John Greenleaf Whittier (1807–93), who lived for some years in Pennsylvania and knew something of the Pennsylvania Dutch and their culture, once referred to Quakers as "nonconductors among the wires." By this he meant that Quakers, following their belief in simplicity, withdrew from complete participation in the culture around them and lived their plain lifestyle away from the world. This included a rejection of weather lore, including Groundhog Day.

Pennsylvania's Quaker farmers usually disapproved of the Pennsylvania Dutch weather beliefs and practices related to certain days in the calendar, all of which they labeled superstition. The Janneys from Bucks County, a Quaker family who moved to Loudoun County, Virginia, took just a bit of Pennsylvania weather lore, and much antilore, with them. One Pennsylvania Dutch superstition opposed by the Quakers was the idea that to get a good flax harvest, the seed should be sown on Good Friday. Quakers had always opposed any celebration of the common religious holidays, believing that all days were equal, none being any holier than the others.

A Quaker relative of the Janneys and a non-Quaker neighbor decided to test the Good Friday notion one year. Both of them got their flax patches ready for planting on Good Friday. However, on that day it poured down rain. The neighbor tramped through the mud and sowed his seed anyway, but the Quaker farmer was away from home, and his sons refused to plant in the rain. When the farmer returned, he was angry about it. In a few days, again in the father's absence, the boys thought they had better plant the flax after all. They wound up with a very good crop, while their neighbor's failed, proving to them that the belief was indeed just superstition.

In these reminiscences, there is a small reference to the Groundhog:

> There was but little of that sort of superstition in our settlement. Farmers generally had an opinion at sunset as to what the following day would be, judging from the sky and the atmosphere [but] the people had no faith in signs and wonders. The ground hog was laughed at and the wet and dry moon was equally in contempt.

Dream Forecasting

Many of our ancestors in Europe and America placed great faith in dreams. Many early Pennsylvania diarists, including Quakers, noted weather in their dreams and checked later to see if their predictions came true.

Some Americans, either seriously or tongue in cheek, consulted the so-called dream books that circulated widely in the eighteenth and nineteenth centuries. One such publication, *The New Dream-Book Interspersed with Stories, Anecdotes, & c.* (1820), gives predictions based on specific weather-related dreams, such as snow, ice, lightning, thunder, floods, and tempests. If a husbandman dreams of snow, for example, this forecasts a good harvest—"that the earth will abound in all things." The outcome is different for merchants and other men of employment, for whom dreaming of snow "signifieth hinderance in their negotiations and voyages." To soldiers, "their designs will be frustrated."

The "Letter from Heaven"

Most Pennsylvania Dutch farm families had a *Himmelsbrief*, or "Letter from Heaven," somewhere in the house. These letters were found all over Western Europe before being brought to Pennsylvania in the eighteenth century. Some were printed in golden letters and framed, a handsome orna-

The Letter from Heaven allegedly protected Pennsylvania Dutch individuals and households from danger, including bad weather. ROUGHWOOD COLLECTION

ment on the wall. But since these documents represented folk religion rather than the official religion of the Protestant churches, others were pasted on the backs of mirrors and thus turned face to the wall. Their powers of protection were still believed to work, even though the text was hidden.

The belief was that the letter, which is supposed to have come directly from God, protected anyone who had it in his house or carried it on his person. Many a Pennsylvania Dutch soldier carried one folded up in a pocket of his uniform, through all our conflicts from the Revolution to the Vietnam War.

One thing that made the letter very special was that in a sense, it supplemented the scriptures, in that it was purportedly an example of postbiblical revelation, or so it was thought. The lengthy text begins with requiring the possessor of it to follow a kind of Protestant version of the Ten Commandments. No one is to work on Sunday, but everyone is to go to church. A kind of Protestant plainness is enjoined, with the command that one is not to adorn the face, not wear "strange hair," and not "carry on arrogance." Persons are advised to give to the poor, not be "ambitious for silver and gold," not carry on "sensualities and desires," and honor father and mother.

While the letter does stress practicing morality, it is full of threats of punishment and damnation:

> I, Jesus, have written this myself with my own hand; he that opposes it and scandalizes, that man shall have to expect no help from me; whoever hath the letter and does not make it known, he is cursed by the Christian Church, and if your sins are as large as they may be, they shall, if you have heartily regretted and repented of them, be forgiven you.
>
> Who does not believe this, he shall die and be punished in hell, and I myself will on the last day inquire after your sins, when you will have to answer me.
>
> And that man who carries this letter with him, and keeps it in his house, no thunder will do him any harm, and he will be safe from fire and water; and he that publishes it to mankind, will receive his reward and a joyful departure from this world.

Because of this last paragraph, which promises protection from thunderstorms and damage by fire and flooding, the document came to be considered a kind of folk insurance policy against natural disasters.

Dozens of editions of this letter were published in German, issuing from the country presses of upstate Dutchland, and dozens of editions of

A LETTER

WRITTEN BY

GOD HIMSELF, AND LEFT DOWN AT MAGDEBURG.

It was written in golden letters, and sent by God through an Angel; to him, who will

copy it, it shall be given; who despiseth it, from him will part

THE LORD.

Whoever works on Sunday, is cursed. Therefore, I command you that you do not work on Sunday, but devotedly go to church; but do not adorn your face; you shall not wear strange hair, and not carry on arrogance; you shall give to the poor of your riches, give plenty and believe, that this letter is written by my own hand and sent out by Christ himself, and that you will not act like the dumb beast; you have six days in the week, during which you shall carry on your labors; but the seventh day (namely, Sunday,) you shall keep holy; if you do not do that, I will send war, famine, pests and death among you, and punish you with many troubles. Also, I command you, every one, whoever he may be, young or old, small and great, that you do not work late on Saturday, but you shall regret your sins, that they may be forgiven you. Do not desire silver and gold; do not carry on sensualities and desires; do think that I have made you and can destroy you.

Do not rejoice when your neighbor is poor, feel moreover sorry with him, then you will fare well.

You, children, honor father and mother, then you will fare well on earth. Who that doth not believe these and holds it, shall be damned and lost. I, Jesus, have written this myself with my own hand; he that opposes it and scandalizes, that man shall have to expect no help from me; whoever hath the lettter and does not make it known, he is cursed by the christian church, and if your sins are as large as they may be, they shall, if you have heartily regretted and repented of them, be forgiven you.

Who does not believe this, he shall die and be punished in hell, and I myself will on the last day inquire after your sins, when you will have to answer me.

And that man who carries this letter with him, and keeps it in his house, no thunder will do him any harm, and he will be safe from fire and water; and he that publishes it to mankind, will receive his reward and a joyful departure from this world.

Do keep my command which I have sent you through my Angel. I, the true God from the heavenly throne, the Son of God and Mary. Amen.

THIS HAS OCCURRED AT MAGDEBURG, IN THE YEAR 1783.

EAGLE JOB PRINT, 542 Penn Street, Reading, Pa.

Letter from Heaven in English, one of many editions issued from local presses in Pennsylvania Dutch Country. ROUGHWOOD COLLECTION

the text appeared in English translation, especially as the use of the High German language dwindled in the twentieth century. Copies still frequently turn up at country sales of Dutch farm property, along with German books (no longer read) and other artifacts of the earlier Dutch culture, like spinning wheels, churns, and flails. Examples have even surfaced where a Sunday School teacher went to the local printer and had an edition run off for his class. In this case, the folk religion and the official religion have joined hands.

The "Fire Letter"

A parallel to the "Letter from Heaven" is the less common, but nevertheless somewhat widespread, *Feuerbrief*, or "Fire Letter," which uses for protective purposes the initials of the Three Wise Men, or Three Holy Kings–C.M.B., for Caspar, Melchior, and Balthasar, the names of the Wise Men according to Catholic tradition. This document is entitled *Ein sehr kräftiges, Heiliges Gebet, Welches zu Cöln am Rhein in goldenen Buchstaben geschrieben und aufgehalten wird*, "A Very Powerful, Holy Prayer, Which Was Written in Golden Letters and Preserved at Cologne on the Rhine."

This letter promises that the Three Wise Men, plus Jesus, Mary, and Joseph, will accompany the bearer wherever he goes and protect him and his companions on the road from thieves, murderers, and evil people, meaning witches. And like the "Letter from Heaven," this letter promises to protect all who carry it with them against sudden death, drowning, and death by fire–hence the common name by which the document is known among the Pennsylvania Dutch.

Furthermore, whoever keeps it in his house will be protected from the plague, from thunder and lightning, and from hailstorms. It also promises pregnant women easy delivery, and if placed in an infant's cradle, it will protect the child from all bewitchment and other misfortune.

The copy reproduced here was published in Kutztown by the printery firm of Urick and Gehring, circa 1875–1880. The entire text is European, but it was republished in several other editions in Pennsylvania, always without a date and, with the exception of this example, without place of publication or publisher. The connection with the city of Cologne (Köln) is important, since Cologne's great cathedral was dedicated to the Three Holy Kings, who according to Matthew 2 followed the star and brought gifts of gold, frankincense, and myrrh to the infant Jesus.

Ein ſehr kräftiges, Heiliges Gebet,

Welches zu Cöln am Rhein in goldenen Buchſtaben geſchrieben und aufbehalten wird.

Heute ſtehe ich auf und neige mich gegen den Tag, in deinem Namen, welchen ich empfangen habe. Der erſte iſt Gott der Vater, † der andere iſt Gott der Sohn, † der dritte iſt Gott der †eilige Geiſt, † der behüte mir mein Leib und Seel, mein Fleiſch und mein Leben, welches mir Jeſus Chriſtus, der Sohn Gottes, ſelber hat gegeben; alſo will ich geſegnet ſeyn wie das heilige Himmel-Brod, daß unſer lieber Herr Jeſus Chriſtus ſeinen Jüngern ſelbſt gegeben hat. Ich gehe aus, und in das Haus über Geſchwöll und Gaſſen, Jeſus † Maria † und Joſeph †, die heiligen drey Könige, Kaſpar †, Melchior † und Balthaſar † ſind meine Weg-Begleiter — der Himmel iſt mein Hut und die Erde meine Schuhe...Dieſe ſechs heiligen Perſonen be leiten mich und alles was ich in meinem Haus habe, und wann ich auf der Straße bin, ſo wollen ſie mich behüten ſammt meinen Ge-

Und wer dies heilige Gebet beten läßt oder höret beten, und bey ſich trägt, der wird nicht des jähen Todes ſterben, noch im Waſſer ertrinken, noch im Feuer verbrennen ; und wer dies heiliges Gebet in ſeinem Hauſe hat, dem kann keine Peſt, weder Donner noch Hagel ſchaden, und wo eine ſchwangere Frau iſt, die in Kindes-Nöthen iſt, und nicht gebären kann, der gebe man dies heilige Gebet in die rechte Hand, oder bete ihr daſſelbe vor, daß ſie es höre, ſo wird ſie von Stund an des Kindes entbunden ; ſo es getauft iſt, lege man dieſes heilige Gebet in die Wiegen, oder henke es demſelben an, ſo wird das Kind von dem Belchreyen und anderem Unglück befreyet ſeyn, dann es ſoll kein Menſch ſeyn, der nicht dieſes Gebet bey ſich trägt, dieweil er vor allen dieſen Nachſtellungen befreyet iſt.

† C. † M † B.

Sancti tres Reges † Caspar † Melchior
† Balthasar, orate
pro nobis nunc & in horris mortis nostrae, Amen.

führten vor Dieb und Mörder, und böſen Leuten, die mir begegnen, die müſſen mich alle lieb und werth haben, dazu verhelfe mir Gott Vater †, Gott der Sohn †, Gott der heilige Geiſt † Jeſus, † Maria † Joſeph, † (Caſpar, Melchior, Balthaſar,) und die vier heiligen Evangeliſten ſeyn mit mir in allen meinem Thun, Handel und Wandel, Geden und Stehen, es ſey auf dem Waſſer oder Land, vor Feuer und Brand, die wollen mich bewahren mit ihrer ſtarken Hand, Gott dem Vater † ergeb ich mich—Gott dem Sohn † befehl ich mich—in Gott den heiligen Geiſt † verſenke ich mich. Die heilige hochgelobte Dreyfaltigkeit ſey ob mir, Jeſus, Maria und Joſeph vor mir, Caſpar, Melchior und Balthaſar ſeyn hinter und vor mir zu allen Zeiten, bis ich komme in die ewige Freud' und Seeligkeit, das helf mir Jeſus, Maria und Joſeph, Amen.

Uriel u. Gehring's Dampfpreſſen-Druck, Kutztown, Pa.

The Fire Letter was believed to protect farm and home from thunder, lightning, and hailstorms, as well as fire. ROUGHWOOD COLLECTION

On Three Kings Day, or *Dreikönig*, January 6, also known in the church calendar as Epiphany, Catholic Rhinelanders and other Germans, Swiss, and Austrians chalk the three initials—now usually K.M.B.—above or on all the doors in their houses to protect all their house space from danger and misfortune.

The Dutch World View

A lifelong student of Pennsylvania Dutch history, religion, and traditions, John Joseph Stoudt, Reformed (UCC) minister and professor, puts all this weather lore into context. In his essay "Pennsylvania German Folklore: An Interpretation," he divides Dutch folklore into five distinct categories, the fifth being "the study of man's place in nature and the world in general: healing, the calendar, the zodiac, omens, weather lore, planting lore, superstitions, beliefs, in short, man's response to the world around him, a shared response." This can be summarized as the Pennsylvania Dutch folk world view, the view they had of the universe, extending from the heavens to the earth, including climate and weather lore. And though Dr. Stoudt did not mention him specifically, the Groundhog is the star of Dutch weather lore.

FESTIVALS AND SOUVENIRS

Punxsutawney Festival/Punxsutawney Phil
    Punxsutawney Area Chamber of Commerce
    124 West Mahoning Street
    Punxsutawney, PA 15767
    (800) 752-7445
    www. punxsutawneychamber.com

For further information on the Groundhog Day event and souvenirs, go to the website of the Punxsutawney Groundhog Club:
    www.groundhog.com

Quarryville Festival/Octoraro Orphie
    Dr. James E. Pennington
    152 Main Street
    New Providence, PA 17560
    (717) 786-3648

To purchase the book, *The Slumbering Groundhog Lodge of Quarryville, Pennsylvania, in the 20th Century,* contact the author:
    Douglas Withers Groff
    P.O. Box 178
    Quarryville, PA 17566

Sun Prairie Festival/Jimmy the Groundhog
    Sun Prairie Chamber of Commerce
    109 East Main Street
    Sun Prairie, WI 53590
    (608) 837-4547
    www.sunprairiechamber.com

Lilburn Festival/Gen. Beauregard Lee
Yellow Game Ranch
4525 Highway 78
Lilburn, GA 30247
(770) 972-6643
www.yellowgameranch.com

Other Festivals
For more information on other Groundhog Day events and prognosticators, go to the website of the Committee for the Commercialization of Groundhog Day:
www.groundhogsday.com

Carols
To order *Groundhog Day Carols,* plus a cassette of the songs, contact:
John and Jan Haigis
1006 Main Street
Darby, PA 19120
(610) 583-0788
www.pasttimespresent.com

BIBLIOGRAPHY

Anderson, Bill. *The True Story of Punxsutawney Phil: A Century of Tradition.* Punxsutawney, Pa.: Spirit Publishing Co., 1997.

Anderson, Bill, et al. *Groundhog Day 1886 to 1992: A Century of Tradition in Punxsutawney, Pennsylvania.* Punxsutawney, Pa.: Spirit Publishing Co., 1992.

Audubon, John James, and John Bachman. *The Viviparous Quadrupeds of North America.* 3 vols. New York: J. J. Audubon, 1846.

Axelrod, Alan, et al. *The Penguin Dictionary of American Folklore.* New York: Penguin Reference, 2000.

Bächtold-Stäubli, Hanns, and Eduard Hoffmann-Krayer, eds. *Handwörterbuch des deutschen Aberglaubens.* Foreword by Christoph Daxelmüller. 2nd ed. 10 vols. Berlin/New York: Walter de Gruyter, 1987.

Barash, D. P. *Marmots: Social Behavior and Ecology.* Stanford, Calif.: Stanford University Press, 1989.

Barba, Preston A., "In Memoriam: Edwin Miller Fogel." *Pennsylvania German Folklore Society* (Yearbook), 14 (1949), 175–181.

———. "Mary Goes over the Mountain." In *'S Pennsylfawnisch Deitsch Eck,* Allentown *Morning Call,* June 29, 1968.

Barba, Preston A., ed. "The Later Poems of John Birmelin." *Pennsylvania German Folklore Society* (Yearbook), 16 (1951).

Barrick, Mac E. "All Signs in Dry Weather Fails." *Keystone Folklore Quarterly* 9:1 (Spring 1964), 23–28.

———. "Moon Signs in Cumberland County." *Pennsylvania Folklife* 15:4 (Summer 1966), 41–43.

Bartlett, John Russell. *Dictionary of Americanisms: A Glossary of Words and Phrases, Usually Regarded as Peculiar to the United States.* New York: Bartlett and Welford, 1848.

Battle, J. H., ed. *History of Columbia and Montour Counties, Pennsylvania.* Chicago: A. Warner, 1887.

Baylor, Frances Courtenay. *Behind the Blue Ridge: A Homely Narrative.* Philadelphia: J. B. Lippincott Co., 1887.

Bense, Johan Frederik. *A Dictionary of the Low-Dutch Element in the English Vocabulary.* The Hague: M. Nijhoff, 1939.

Bergen, Fanny D., and W. W. Newell. "Weather-Lore." *Journal of American Folk-Lore* 2 (1889), 203–8.

Black, Brian. "Finding Meaning in Phil's Shadow." *Altoona Mirror,* January 21, 2001.

Blackburn, Bonnie, and Leofranc Holford-Stevens. *The Oxford Companion to the Year.* New York: Oxford University Press, 1999.

Boehm, Carole, ed. *The Night Mayor from Kitchen to Parlor: Get to Know What Good Is!* Reading, Pa.: Unitarian Universalist Church, 1975.

Boehme, Sarah E. *John James Audubon in the West: The Last Expedition, Mammals of North America.* New York: Harry N. Abrams, in association with the Buffalo Bill Historical Society, 2000.

Brand, John. *Observations on Popular Antiquities.* New Castle upon Tyne: J. Johnson, 1777.

Brendle, Thomas R. "Customs of the Year in the Dutch Country." *Pennsylvania Dutchman* 3:12 (November 15, 1951), 1, 7.

Brendle, Thomas R., and William S. Troxell. *Pennsylvania German Folk Tales, Legends, Once-upon-a-time Stories, Maxims, and Sayings Spoken in the Dialect Popularly Known as Pennsylvania Dutch.* Pennsylvania German Society, 50 (1944).

——. "Pennsylvania German Songs." In George Korson, ed. *Pennsylvania Songs and Legends.* Philadelphia: University of Pennsylvania Press, 1949, 62–128.

Brickell, John. *The Natural History of North Carolina.* Dublin: J. Carson, 1737.

Brunvand, Jan Harold, ed. *American Folklore: An Encyclopedia.* New York: Garland Publishing, 1996.

Bryant, Jim. *The Wild Game and Fish Cookbook.* Boston: Little, Brown, 1984.

Carpenter, Rhys. *Folk Tale, Fiction and Saga in the Homeric Epics.* Sather Classical Lectures, University of California, vol. 20. Berkeley/Los Angeles: University of California, 1946.

Chambers, R. *The Book of Days: A Miscellany of Popular Antiquities in Connection with the Calendar.* Philadelphia: J. B. Lippincott & Co., 1863.

Ciavaglia, Jo. "Following by Example." Levittown *Courier-Times,* February 3, 2000.

"Clymer H. Freas Dies in Tampa, Fla., after long Illness: Former City Editor of the Spirit Who Brought Punx'y Groundhog Fame." Punxsutawney *Spirit,* October 22, 1947.

Cox, Harvey. *The Feast of Fools: A Theological Essay on Festivity and Fantasy.* New York: Harper and Row, 1970.

Crissey, Mike. "Punxy Phil Sees Shadow; A Lot of People See Him." *Altoona Mirror,* February 3, 2001.

Cummings, John M. "Steps to Take about Groundhog Roasting." *Philadelphia Inquirer* [1960s].

Cumont, Franz. *Astrology and Religion among the Greeks and Romans.* London: Constable and Co., 1912.

Darlington, William, comp. "Pennsylvania Weather Records, 1644–1835." *Pennsylvania Magazine of History and Biography* 15 (1891): 109–112.

Davidson, H. R. Ellis. *Myth and Symbols in Pagan Europe: Early Scandinavian and Celtic Religions.* Syracuse, N.Y.: Syracuse University Press, 1988.

Davis, Christopher R. "Totemism and Civic Boosterism in Punxsutawney, Pennsylvania, 1899–1909." *Western Pennsylvania Historical Magazine* 18 (1935), 101–130.

de Vfies, Jan. *Keltische Religion.* Stuttgart: W. Kohlhammer, 1961.

De Voe, Thomas F. *The Market Assistant: Containing a Brief Description of Every Article of Human Food Sold in the Public Markets of the Cities of New York, Boston, Philadelphia, and Brooklyn; Including the Various Domestic and Wild*

Animals, Poultry, Game, Fish, Vegetables, Fruits, &c., &c. with Many Curious Incidents and Anecdotes. New York: Orange Judd and Company, 1866; Preface dated 1854. Groundhog, 129–130.

Donner, William W. "Loss Uns Deitcha Wos M'r Sin. Leave Us Dutch the Way We Are: The Grundsow Lodges." [Kutzton University] *Pennsylvania German Review* (Spring 2002), 39–57.

Dorson, Richard M. *Buying the Wind: Regional Folklore in the United States.* Chicago: University of Chicago Press, 1964.

Drake, Milton. *Almanacs of the United States.* New York: Scarecrow Press, 1962.

Druckenbrod, Richard. "Groundhog Lodge Enjoys Spring Versammling." Allentown *Morning Call*, March 31, 1988.

Dunwoody, Henry Harrison Chase. *Weather Proverbs.* U.S. Signal Office, *Signal Service Notes* series, no. 9. Washington, D. C.: Government Printing Office, 1883.

Eckstein, James A. "Observance of Holidays in Southeastern Pennsylvania." *Pennsylvania Dutchman* 3:3 (June 1, 1952), 3, 8.

Elkin, James. *Snyder Family of Dora, Pennsylvania.* 1999.

Erich, Oswald A., and Richard Beitl. *Wörterbuch der Deutschen Volkskunde.* 3rd ed. Edited by Richard Beitl with the assistance of Klaus Beitl. Stuttgart: Alfred Kröner Verlag, 1974.

Fergus, Chuck. *Wildlife of Pennsylvania and the Northeast.* Mechanicsburg, Pa.: Stackpole Books, 2000.

"Fersammlinge." *American-German Review* 14 (June–August 1947), 24.

Fleck, Jon. "Punxy Phil Loved, but Family Is Not." *Altoona Mirror*, February 2, 2003.

Flexner, Stuart Berg, and Anne H. Soukhanor. *Speaking Freely: A Guided Tour of American English from Plymouth Rock to Silicon Valley.* New York: Oxford Univeristy Press, 1997.

Flood, Barbara. *Game in the Kitchen: Cooking for Nimrods, Anglers, and Their Friends.* Barre, Mass.: Barre Publishers, 1968.

Fogel, Edwin M. *Beliefs and Superstitions of the Pennsylvania Germans.* Philadelphia: Americana Germanica Press, 1915.

———. "Of Months and Days." *Pennsylvania German Folklore Society* (Yearbook) 5 (1940).

Francis, Naila. "Progress Patty Mirrors Phil's Predictions." Levittown *Courier-Times*, February 3, 2000.

French, Trapper Jack. *Pioneer Heritage Wild Game Cookbook: Old-Fashioned Frontier Favorites.* Jupiter, Fla.: Realco Publishing, 1986.

Freed, Judy C., and Terry A. Fye, eds. *The Unofficial Groundhogese Dictionary and Other Well-Known and Unknown Weather Facts and Fiction.* Punxsutawney, Pa.: Spirit Publishing Co., 1994.

Futhey, J. Smith, and Gilbert Cope. *History of Chester County, Pennsylvania.* Philadelphia: William H. Everts, 1881.

Fye, Terry. "In the Hometown Kitchen: Groundhog Punxsy Style." *Hometown Punxsutawney*, February 2002.

Gass, Patrick. *A Journal of the Voyages and Travels of a Corps of Discovery, under the Command of Capt. Lewis and Capt. Clarke.* Pittsburgh, 1807.

Gerhard, Elmer S. "Pennsylvania German Folk Lore." *Perkiomen Region* 9:3 (1931), 87–96.

Geschwindt, Don F. "Holidays in the Dutch Country." *Pennsylvania Dutchman* 2:21 (April 1, 1951), 3, 8.

Gilbert, Bill. "A Groundhog's 'Day' Means More to Us Than It Does to Him." *Smithsonian Magazine* 16 (February 1985), 60–68.

Gilbert, Glenn G., ed. *The German Language in America: A Symposium.* Austin/London: University of Texas Press, 1971.

Gilbert, Russell W. *Bilder un Gedanke: A Book of Pennsylvania German Verse.* Pennsylvania German Society (new series) 9 (1975).

——. "The Oratory of the Pennsylvania Germans at the Versammlinge." *Susquehanna University Studies* 4 (1951): 187–213.

——. "Versammling Speeches." *Pennsylvania Speech Annual* 13 (1956): 3–20.

Gillespie, Angus K. *Folklorist of the Coal Fields: George Korson's Life and Work.* University Park, Pa.: Pennsylvania State University Press, 1980.

——. "Pennsylvania Folk Festivals in the 1930s." *Pennsylvania Folklife* 26:1 (Fall 1976), 2–11.

Glass, Marvin. *What Happened Today, Freddy Groundhog?* New York: Crown Publishers, 1989.

Glimm, James York. *Flat-Landers and Ridge-Runners: Folktales from the Mountains of Northern Pennsylvania.* Pittsburgh: University of Pittsburgh Press, 1983.

Godman, John Davidson. *American Natural History.* 3 vols. Philadelphia: H. C. Carey and I. Lea, 1826–28.

Gotthard, P. *Rigyberg der Himmelsköniginn eingeweiht unter dem Titel: Maria zum Schnee.* Zug, Switzerland: Joh. Michael Aloys Binnschi, 1802.

Graeff, Arthur D. "Astrology in Pennsylvania-German Almanacs." *American-German Review* 5:6 (August 1939), 24–29.

——. "Weather Prophecies in Pennsylvania-German Almanacs." *American-German Review* 6:6 (August 1940), 10–14.

Grimes, David. "Is Punxy Phil Next Terrorist Target?" *Altoona Mirror*, February 1, 2002.

Groff, Douglas Withers. *The Slumbering Groundhog Lodge of Quarryville, Pennsylvania in the 20th Century.* Lancaster, Pa.: Whitmore Printing and Typesetting, 2000.

"Groundhog Day." *Encyclopedia Britannica Micropedia.* 1988 ed.

"Groundhog Day." *What's Happening Now in Lancaster County and Environs* 4:10 (January 1977).

"Groundhog Gives Chilly Forecast." *Reading Eagle*, February 3, 2002.

"Groundhog Is Better Eater Than Prophet." *Altoona Mirror*, February 28, 1962.

Gutch, Eliza. *Folk-Lore Concerning the North Riding of Yorkshire, York and the Ainsty.* London: D. Nutt, 1901.

Haigis, John and Jan. *Groundhog Day Carols: A Selection of Songs by John and Jan Haigis, Celebrating This Special Time of Year.* Philadelphia: The Marvelous Megalethoscope, 1997.

Hand, Wayland D., ed. *Popular Beliefs and Superstitions from North Carolina.* The Frank C. Brown Collection of North Carolina Folklore, Vol. 7. Durham, N.C.: Duke University Press, 1964.

Harlan, Richard. *Fauna Americana: Being a Description of the Mammiferous Animals Inhabiting North America.* Philadelphia: Anthony Finley, 1825.

Harris, Jeff. "Shortcuts—The World of the Woodchuck (*Marmota monax*)." *Altoona Mirror*, January 29, 2001.

Hazlitt, W. Carew. *Faiths and Folklore: A Dictionary of National Beliefs, Superstitions and Popular Customs. Past and Current, with Their Classical and For-*

eign Analogues, Described and Illustrated. 2 vols. London: Reeves and Turner, 1905.

Henneberger, George F. "Weather Lore in Franklin County." *Pennsylvania Dutchman* 3:16 (January 15, 1952), 3.

Hoch, Herman E. *The Groundhog's Prophecy for 1905.* [Lancaster]: privately printed, 1905.

——. *The Groundhog's Prophecy for 1906.* [Lancaster]: privately printed, 1906.

Hodel, Janet. "Rain Day in Waynesburg, Pennsylvania." *Pennsylvania Folklife* 25:1 (Autumn 1975), 20–23.

Hodges, Leigh Mitchell. "The Town Where the Groundhog Grows: Punx'y Launches Luscious Prophet as National Dish." Philadelphia *North American,* September 5, 1909.

Hoffman, W. J. "Folk-Lore of the Pennsylvania Germans." *Journal of American Folk-Lore* 1 (1888): 125–35; 2 (1889): 23–35, 191–202.

——. "Popular Superstitions." *Pennsylvania German Society* 5 (1895), 70–81.

Howells, William. *The Heathens: Primitive Man and His Religions.* Garden City, N. Y.: Anchor Books, Doubleday & Co., 1962.

Humphreys, W. J. *Rainmaking and Other Weather Vagaries.* Baltimore: Williams and Wilkins Co., 1926.

——. *Ways of Weather.* Lancaster, Pa.: Jaques Cattell Press, 1942.

Hurst, David. "40,000 Phil Fans Fill Knob." *Altoona Mirror,* February 3, 2003.

Huntley, George William, Jr. *A Story of the Sinnamahone.* Williamsport, Pa.: Williamsport Printing & Binding Co., 1936.

Irmscher, Christoph, ed. *John James Audubon: Writings and Drawings.* Library of America Series. New York: Penguin Putnam, 1999.

Janney, Asa Moore, and Werner L. Janney, eds. *John Jay Janney's Virginia: An American Farm Lad's Life in the Early 19th Century.* McLean, Va.: EPM Publications, 1978.

Kemp, A. F. "The Pennsylvania German Versammlinge." *Pennsylvania German Folklore Society* (Yearbook) 9 (1944): 187–218.

Kennedy, Craig. *Pennsylvania Fairs and Country Festivals.* Mechanicsburg, Pa.: Stackpole Books, 1996.

Kenney, William H., III. "Jacob Taylor and His Almanacs." *Pennsylvania Folklife* 14:3 (Spring 1965), 32–35.

Kenton, Warren. *Astrology: The Celestial Mirror.* London: Thames and Hudson, 1974.

Kittredge, George Lyman. *The Old Farmer and His Almanac.* Cambridge, Mass.: Harvard University Press, 1920.

Knohr, E. L. "Customs and Beliefs in South-Eastern Pennsylvania Concerning the Holidays of the Year." *Pennsylvania Dutchman* 2:20 (March 15, 1951), 5–7.

Korson, George. *Black Rock: Mining Folklore of the Pennsylvania Dutch.* Publications of the Pennsylvania German Society, vol. 59. Baltimore: The Johns Hopkins Press, 1960.

——. *Pennsylvania Songs and Legends.* Philadelphia: University of Pennsylvania Press, 1949.

Koscielniak, Bruce. *Geoffrey Groundhog Predicts the Weather.* Boston: Houghton Mifflin Co., 1995.

Kring, Hilda Adam. "Mary Goes over the Mountain." *Pennsylvania Folklife* 19:4 (Summer 1970): 54–60.

Kroll, Steven. *It's Groundhog Day!* Illustrated by Jeni Bassett. New York: Holiday House, 1987.

Kulp, Isaac Clarence, Jr. "E' Bissel Fun Dem un e' Bissel Fun Sellem (A Little Bit of This and a Little Bit of That)." *Goschenhoppen Region* 1:3 (Lichtmess 1969), 7–8.

Leavy, Thomas A. "A Comparative Analysis of Pittsburgh Weather (1885–1886 to 1971–1972." *Western Pennsylvania Historical Magazine* 57 (January 1974), 123–26.

LeRoux, Françoise. *Les Fêtes Celtiques.* Rennes: Ouest-France, 1995.

Letowsky, Ruth, et al. "Beau to Prophesy Weather and Meaning of Life." Press release, Yellow River Game Ranch, Lilburn, Georgia, January 28, 2003.

Levine, Abby. *Gretchen Groundhog, It's Your Day!* Illustrated by Nancy Cote. Morton Grove, Ill.: Albert Whitman and Co., 1978.

Lewerenz, Dan. "Love, Not Weather, May Be on Prognosticator's Mind." *Altoona Mirror*, January 29, 2003.

Lifshin, Sarah M. "York Groundhogs Split on Forecast." *York Sunday News*, February 3, 2002.

Light, Elaine. *People Who Love Groundhogs: Stories of Punxsutawney and Its People.* Punxsutawney, Pa.: Spirit Publishing Co., 1982.

Light, Elaine Kahn, and Ruth B. Hamill, eds. *Cooking with the Groundhog.* Compiled by the Adrian Hospital Auxiliary of Punxsutawney. Sykesville, Pa.: Nupp Printing Co., 1958; 9th printing, June 1999.

MacKillop, James. *Dictionary of Celtic Mythology.* Oxford/New York: Oxford University Press, 1998.

MacNeill, Máire. *The Feast of Lughnasa.* Oxford: Oxford University Press, 1962.

Mathews, Mitford M., ed. *A Dictionary of Americanisms on Historical Principles.* Chicago: University of Chicago Press, 1951.

McKnight, William James. *Jefferson County, Pennsylvania: Her Pioneers and People, 1800–1915.* 2 vols. Chicago: J. H. Beers, 1917.

Miller, Daniel, ed. *Pennsylvania German: A Collection of Pennsylvania German Productions in Poetry and Prose.* Vol. 1. 2nd ed. Reading, Pa.: Daniel Miller, 1904.

Miller, Richard K.. *Pennsylvania German Groundhog Lodges: The Origin of Pennsylvania German Groundhog Lodges.* Kutztown, Pa.: Pennsylvania German Cultural Heritage Center, Kutztown University, 1997.

Neff, Larry M., ed. "Selections from Arthur Graeff's Scholla." *Publications of the Pennsylvania German Society* 5 (1971).

Neuberger, Hans H., and F. Briscol Stephens. *Weather and Man.* Englewood Cliffs, N.J.: Prentice-Hall, 1948.

Oda, Wilbur H. "The Himmelsbrief." *Pennsylvania Dutchman* 1:21 (December 1949): 3.

O'Toole, Christine H. "Festivals Highlight Animal Magnetism." *Pittsburgh Post-Gazette*, February 3, 2002.

Owens, Frances E. *Mrs. Owens' Cook Book and Useful Household Hints. Revised and Illustrated. To Which Has Been Added a Farmers' Department Containing Much Valuable Information. And There Has Been Still Further Added Chapters on Lunches and Luncheons, Potential Energy of Food, Chafing Dish Cookery, and Translations of French Terms in Modern Menus.* Chicago: American Publishing House, ©1884, 1903.

Owens, J. G. "Folk-Lore from Buffalo Valley, Central Pennsylvania." *Journal of American Folk-Lore* 4 (1891), 115–128.

Palmatier, Robert A. *Speaking of Animals: A Dictionary of Animal Metaphors.* Westport, Conn.: Greenwood Press, 1995.

Peattie, Roderick. *The Great Smokies and the Blue Ridge*. New York: Vanguard Press, 1943.

Pound, Louise. *Nebraska Folklore*. Lincoln: University of Nebraska Press, 1959.

Pulling, Anne Frances. *Images of America: Around Punxsutawney*. Charleston, S. C.: Arcadia Publishing/Tempus Publishing, 2001.

"Rain Day: Waynesburg's Claim to Fame." In *Waynesburg, Pennsylvania, Area Chamber of Commerce*. Waynesburg, Pa.: Village Profile, 2002.

Reichard, Harry Hess. *Pennsylvania German Dialect Writings and Their Writers*. Pennsylvania German Society 26 (1918).

———. *Pennsylvania German Verse*. Pennsylvania German Society 48 (1940).

Reichmann, Felix. "Groundhog Day." *American-German Review* 9 (February 1942), 11–13.

Rhoads, Collier. "Pennsylvania German Groundhog Lodges." *Keystone Folklore Quarterly* 7–9. Reprinted from the Norristown *Times-Herald*.

Rhoads, Samuel N. *The Mammals of Pennsylvania and New Jersey*. Philadelphia: self-published, 1903.

Richter, Conrad. *Over the Blue Mountain*. New York: Alfred A. Knopf, 1967.

Riemerman, Paul A. "A Manner of Speaking: Grundsow Lodsch Meets to Salute German Traditions." Doylestown *Intelligencer-Record*, January 28, 1990.

Rohart, Mia. "Shadow of Things to Come: Couples Take the Plunge on Punxsy's Special Day." *Altoona Mirror*, February 2, 2001.

Rosenberger, Homer Tope. *The Pennsylvania Germans, 1891–1965 (Frequently Known as the "Pennsylvania Dutch"); Seventy-Fifth Anniversary Volume of the Pennsylvania German Society*. Vol. 63. Lancaster, Pa.: Pennsylvania German Society, 1966.

Sachse, Julius Friedrich. "Old-Time Home Superstitions." *Pennsylvania-German* 8 (1907), 389–99.

———. "Popular Beliefs and Superstitions." *Lancaster County Historical Society* 7 (1903), 75–101.

Santino, Jack. *All around the Year: Holidays and Celebrations in American Life*. Urbana: University of Illinois Press, 1994.

Sartori, Paul. *Westfälische Volkskunde*. 2nd rev. ed. Leipzig: Quelle & Meyer, 1929.

Schrijnen, Jos. *Nederlandsche Volkskunde*. 2 vols. Zutphen: W. J. Thieme & Cie., n. d.

Scott, Kate M. *History of the One Hundred and Fifth Regiment of Pennsylvania Volunteers: A Complete History of the Organization, Marches, Battles, Toils, and Dangers Participated in by the Regiment, from the Beginning to the Close of the War, 1861–1865*. Philadelphia: New World Publishing Co., 1877.

Semmel, David. "Bruder Grundsow Gelobt am Fimf un Sechzischt Yairlich Fersommling: Brother Groundhog Honored at 65th Yearly Gathering." *Parkland and Northwestern Press*, February 8, 2001.

———. "The Groundhog: King of Pa. German Weather Lore, Patron Saint of Lehigh Valley Grundsow Lodges." *Parkland and Northwestern Press*, January 24–30, 2000.

———. "Grundsow Wedder Brofeet, Sauergraut un Gschpass: Groundhog Weather Forecasting, Sauerkraut and Fun." *Parkland and Northwestern Press*, March 20–26, 2000.

———. "The Lechaw Dawl Grundsow Weather Predictions: The Real Thing, Not a Wild Party Like at Punxsutawney." *Parkland and Northwestern Press*, February 7–13, 2000.

Shoemaker, Alfred L. "Pumpernickle Bill: Dialect Writer." *Pennsylvania Dutch-man* 1:4 (May 26, 1949), 1.

Shoemaker, Alfred L., ed. "Folklore from the Diary of James L. Morris, 1845–1846." *Pennsylvania Dutchman* 3:17 (February 1, 1952), 2.

——. "Of Folkloristic Interest." *Pennsylvania Dutchman* 4:13 (March 1, 1953): 4, 5, 14.

Smart, Peter. *Vanitie and Downefall of Superstitious Popish Ceremonies.* [London], 1628.

Smith, Elmer Lewis, John G. Stewart, and M. Ellsworth Kyger. "The Pennsylvania Germans of the Shenandoah Valley." *Pennsylvania German Folklore Society* (Yearbook) 26 (1962), Allentown, Pa., 1964.

Snyder, Robert L. "The Pennsylvania Woodchuck." Harrisburg, Pa.: Pennsylvania Game Commision, [1969].

Solomon, Wendy. "The Shadow Knows: Now More Than Ever, People Need the Revelry of Groundhog Day." Allentown *Morning Call*, February 3, 2002.

Story, M. L. "The Old Family Almanac." *Southern Folklore Quarterly* 23 (1959), 233–38.

Stoudt, John Baer. "Weather Prognostications and Superstitions among the Pennsylvania Germans." *Pennsylvania German* 6 (1905): 328–36; 7 (1906): 242–43.

Stoudt, John Joseph. "Pennsylvania German Folklore: An Interpretation." *Pennsylvania German Folklore Society* (Yearbook) 14 (1951), Allentown, Pa., 1953.

Swainson, C. *Handbook of Weather Folk-Lore.* Edinburgh/London: W. Blackwood & Sons, 1873.

Tappolet, Walter, and Albert Ebneter. *Das Marienlob der Reformatoren.* Tübingen: Ketzmann-Verlag, 1967.

Thompson, Leon. "Groundhog Legends." [Mount Joy] *Antiques & Auction News* 20:4 (January 27, 1989), 1, 8.

Tolksdorf, Ulrich. *Volksleben in den Ermländersiedlungen der Eifel.* Marburg: N. G. Elwert Verlag, 1967.

Troutman, Carrie Haas. "Pioneer Days in Mahantongo Valley." In *'S Pennsyl-fawnisch Deitsch Eck,* Allentown *Morning Call,* October 9, 1948.

Troxell, William S. "The First Grundsow Lodge." *Pennsylvania Dutchman* 4:12 (February 15, 1953), reprinted from the Allentown *Morning Call,* and appearing in Donner, 48–49.

Trumbore, Mark S. *A Superficial Collection of Penna. German Erotic Folklore* Pennsburg, Pa.: Privately published, 1978.

van Gennep, Arnold. *The Rites of Passage.* Chicago: University of Chicago Press, 1960.

Wallace, Anthony F. C. *Religion: An Anthropological View.* New York: Random House, 1966.

Weaver, William Woys. *Sauer's Herbal Cures: America's First Book of Botanic Healing, 1762–1778.* New York: Routledge, 2001.

Webster's New International Dictionary of the English Language. 2nd ed. Springfield, Mass.: J. & C. Merriam Co., 1938.

Weiser, Francis X. *Handbook of Christian Feasts and Customs.* New York: Harcourt, Brace and Co., 1952.

Whitaker, John C., Jr., Robert Elman, and Carol Nehring. *The Audubon Society Field Guide to North American Mammals.* New York: Alfred A. Knopf, Borzoi Books, 1980.

Whitney, Annie Westin, and Caroline Canfield Bullock, collectors. *Folk-Lore from Maryland*. New York: American Folk-Lore Society, 1925.

Williams, Candice. "Ground Hog Lodge Meets: Group Strives to Keep Pennsylvania German Culture Alive." Quakertown *Free Press*, January 31, 2002.

Wilson, Don E., and Sue Ruff, eds. *The Smithsonian Book of North American Mammals*. Washington/London: Smithsonian Institution Press, in association with the American Society of Mammalogists, 1999.

Winkler, Louis. "Pennsylvania German Astronomy and Astrology." *Pennsylvania Folklife* 21–24 (1970–73).

Wolff, Dick. "A Good Recipe for Braised Woodchuck." Valley View *Citizen-Standard*, April 24, 1992.

Wood, Anthony R. "More Winter Hinges on Air Patterns, Not Groundhog's Shadow." *Philadelphia Inquirer*, February 2, 2001.

Worden, Amy. "Phil the Would-Be Media Star Casts a Thin Shadow in New York." *Philadelphia Inquirer*, February 3, 2001.

Yoder, Don. *Discovering American Folklife: Essays on Folk Culture and the Pennsylvania Dutch*. Mechanicsburg, Pa.: Stackpole Books, 2001.

——. "Gifts of the Pennsylvania Dutch." *The World & I* 3:11 (November 1988), 642–53.

——. "Kutztown and America." *Pennsylvania Folklife* 14:4 (Summer 1965).

——. "Pennsylvania German Folklore Research: A Historical Analysis." In *The German Language in America: A Symposium*, edited by Glenn G. Gilbert, 70–105. Austin: University of Texas Press, 1971. See also "German Folklore in America: Discussion," 148–163.

——. "The Pennsylvania Germans: Three Centuries of Identity Crisis." In *America and the Germans*, edited by Frank Trommler and Joseph McVeigh, vol. 1, 40–65. Philadelphia: University of Pennsylvania Press, 1985.

——. "Symposium on Folk Religion." *Western Folklore* 33:1 (January 1974), 1–87. See especially "Toward a Definition of Folk Religion," 2–15; and "Introductory Bibliography on Folk Religion," 16–34.

——. "Die Volkslieder der Pennsylvanien-Deutschen." In *Handbuch des Volksliedes*, edited by Rolf Wilhelm Brednich et al., vol. 2, 221–70. Munich: Wilhelm Fink, 1975.

Yoder, Don, and Thomas E. Graves. *Hex Signs: Pennsylvania Dutch Barn Decorations and Their Meaning*. 2nd ed. Mechanicsburg, Pa.: Stackpole Books, 2000.

Yoder, Elmer S. *I Saw It in THE BUDGET*. Hartville, Ohio: Diakonia Ministries, 1990.

Zervanos, Stam M. "Timing of Hibernation Immergence and Emergence in Woodchucks (*Marmota monax*)." In *Adaptive Strategies and Diversity in Marmots*, edited by R. Ramousse et al., International Network on Marmots, 157–64.

Zervanos, Stam M., and Carmen M. Salsbury. "Seasonal Body Temperature Fluctuations and Energetic Strategies in Free-Ranging Eastern Woodchucks (*Marmota monax*)." *Journal of Mammalogy* 84 (2003), 299–310.

Zurcher, Neil. *Ohio Oddities: A Guide to the Curious Attractions of the Buckeye State*. Cleveland: Gray & Co., 2001.

INDEX